IT IS NOT HOW LIFE STARTS, IT IS HOW YOU FINISH IT

A SURVIVOR'S GUIDE TO PEACE AND HAPPINESS

Jane Bowden

It Is Not How Life Starts, It Is How You Finish It

i

Dedication

For my children — your love gave me the strength to
fight, to heal, and to rise.

For the girl I once was — silenced, afraid, and unseen.
You made it. I see you now.

For every survivor who has ever felt invisible, ashamed, or
alone — you are not broken. You are brave.

For my mum — carrying your own burdens and surviving
your own trauma, even in silence.

To those who tried to break me — you failed.

And to everyone who has ever felt shattered — this is how
we rise.

Acknowledgement

To Harold Smith—my editor, and friend. Through the British-proofreading company.

Also my sister Suzanne.

However I would like to express my deepest gratitude to the Finest Book Publishers for their support, guidance, and belief in my work. Your dedication made this journey not only possible but also truly enjoyable.

About the Author

Jane Bowden is a survivor, a mother, and a passionate advocate for healing and resilience. She holds a First-Class Honours degree in Nursing and has devoted her life to caring for others — even while navigating and overcoming her own deeply personal challenges.

Jane finds peace in nature, solace in music, and strength through meditation and spiritual reflection. She enjoys coffee, laughter, and the beauty of a simple life. Though she was never allowed to learn French as a child, she dreams of traveling and exploring new languages and cultures.

She lives in the UK, surrounded by her loving family, grounded in hope and purpose.

It Is Not How Life Starts, It Is How You

Finish It

Contents

Jane Bowden

It Is Not How Life Starts, It Is How You

Finish It

Page Left Blank Intentionally

Chapter 1: The Silence Behind Smiles

This book delves into the devastating effects of child sexual, mental, and physical abuse—told through the eyes of a survivor. It is my life story, filled with ups and downs, showing that survival is possible and thriving is within reach.

I believe love and forgiveness are the true sources of strength, and I have discovered that positivity is the key to happiness. But make no mistake—overcoming the trauma of child sexual abuse is an uphill battle. Perhaps one of the hardest. No one talks about it. Or at least, they didn't when it happened to me. Support was scarce, silence was the norm, and the wounds ran deep. True forgiveness is about freeing yourself, not excusing the actions of others.

Abuse doesn't just destroy one life, it sends shockwaves through families, relationships, and futures. Every news report of another case reminds me of the long-lasting pain survivors endure. Society gasps in horror before moving on, but the children? They are left with scars, memories, and lifelong battles.

This is my journey. And for those who have suffered, know this: you are not just another statistic. You can heal. You can find strength. And you are never alone.

There will be books to follow, chronicling the path to self-love, empowerment, and ultimate fulfilment. Don't get me wrong, healing is undeniably difficult, but it is not impossible.

I have struggled when the news reports cases of paedophiles. People feel sorry for abused children in that moment—their compassion runs high, and they say it is disgusting. However, as soon as the newsreel finishes, they stop thinking about that child. The child becomes just another statistic.

The child who may or may not have seen their mum or dad arguing and hitting each other and may have even endured sexual advances—full sexual intercourse, or being told to do things with their hands that they were not comfortable with.

Having been a victim of sexual abuse, I would have preferred my parents to talk to me when I was little about the possibility of someone touching me where I did not like—in my private areas under my knickers, under my bra, or in that area before I even had a bra—rather than enduring the experience of being sexually exploited until I reached the age of fifteen.

This might be difficult to hear, but it was just as raw to experience, being touched by my own grandfather. Discovering that your child has been sexually abused by a family member or a trusted family friend is an unimaginable, devastating experience. The painful truth is that children are more likely to suffer abuse at the hands of someone they know rather than a stranger. If you were to find out that your child had been harmed by a pervert, your world would likely fall apart. You might wish you had been more aware, more cautious, and less trusting.

I was fortunate to seek help. At eighteen, I went to my GP and pursued counselling. Through therapy, I learned a powerful truth: knowledge is power. Protecting children isn't about sheltering them or restricting their experiences; it's about equipping them with knowledge, confidence, and the ability to safeguard themselves. When children understand their rights and boundaries from an early age, they are better prepared to navigate the world safely.

Our children are our future.

The only way to change the future and stop this abuse from happening is by taking action. Many people feel frustration and anger when paedophiles receive their prison sentences. Yet, once the conversation shifts, they leave it to the judicial system to deliver justice and remove abusers from society.

But true change doesn't come from punishment alone. It comes from prevention, from education, from arming our children with knowledge and the confidence to protect themselves. It comes from speaking up, even when it's uncomfortable.

We must do more.

We need to change this, and it "starts and ends with us". Let's stop the silence at least. Discuss the subject openly, without treating it as taboo.

From my personal experience, children do not always speak up. To me, my grandfather's behaviour was normal. I did not know it was wrong because he had always done it. So, children may not necessarily tell their caregiver about their relative touching them for example an uncle, aunty, cousin, sibling or any family member had been touching them inappropriately because they may have thought it was normal and not an abuse. They might have been manipulated in a sophisticated manner similar to my experience, which could explain their silence. Not necessarily out of threats but out of feeling somehow to blame! Despite the many dangers lurking online, abuse is still more likely to happen right under your nose.

That's why I am here. I set out to write this book, to speak out as a survivor of sexual abuse. It has been a difficult journey, not only in developing this book but also in figuring out how to begin. My goal is to support, comfort, and help others who have endured the same vile experience. By reading this book, I hope you will gain insight into the difficulties and challenges I have faced, battling isolation, loneliness, and the weight of my own thoughts.

If you are struggling, I want you to know that your story can change through hope. Every story has the potential for transformation, and that begins with understanding and the courage to talk about these experiences with friends and family, free from fear or judgement. My hope is that every reader realises we are all incredible human beings, capable of overcoming even the darkest adversities with love, compassion, and positivity.

Most importantly, this book is about positivity. It is about showing you that you have the power to change your story. By sharing my thoughts, emotions, and struggles, I hope that any survivors reading this, especially those grappling with the same challenges, will understand that what they feel is normal. I want them to know they are not alone. The shame and fear they may carry are not reflections of who they are, but rather symptoms of the abuse they endured. This book also aims to show that when you are treated abnormally, your reactions will not always be 'normal', and that is okay. Even after all these years, I still feel moments of shame and hesitation when speaking about my past, fearing judgement. Yet, despite that, I truly believe I have healed. My life is filled with richness, love, and beautiful people. The journey has been long, but I have learned to give myself love and gratitude. Through the power of positive thinking, I have reached this point in my life. It is a process, a lifelong journey, but meditation and self-reflection have played a crucial role in my healing. When we face our fears, we create the possibility for change.

By standing up and speaking out, we can help protect future generations. The conversation should not be limited to dealing with abusers after the fact, but rather focused on preventing abuse from happening in the first place. We need to educate parents on what to look for, how to listen to their children, and how to create environments where abuse cannot thrive. Remember, perpetrators are cowards. They manipulate because they feel inadequate and seek control through deception. But knowledge, awareness, and open conversations can strip them of their power. It's time to take a stand, not just for ourselves, but for the safety of every child.

This book is to show that you, like I did, can overcome and flourish! However, it is not easy, and it will be very difficult at times. Although I can tell you, my friends, that it is worth every struggle, every disappointment, and every failed attempt you may experience on the journey.

We can change the world by taking back our power, the power to change our lives, the power to stop the perverted abuser from ruining them. They took your past; do not allow them to take your future. Make it bright, make it right. Take back control by learning to pour into yourself. Meditation allowed me to connect with my spiritual side, which has helped immensely. Although, that has only been since the past year.

My children were thankfully not abused because I unfortunately could not unknow what I knew. I found parenting very difficult for so many reasons. Firstly, I had, had a dysfunctional childhood and saw my father hit my mum and also, I knew he cheated on her. Then I had my grandad who would want me to have sexual encounter with him and expect to use my body as a vessel. For when it suited him. With the abuse and confusion, I did not know what to do. I did not do well at school, and I was actually misdiagnosed with learning difficulties at a young age. This caused me so much hardship and anguish.

It Is Not How Life Starts, It Is How You
Finish It

Most people raise their children instinctively, following the patterns set by their own parents. But having grown up in a dysfunctional home, I couldn't do that. Every action, every decision had to be carefully thought through, I was determined not to repeat the cycle. I was fortunate to receive counselling at eighteen, where I learned about the danger of repeating destructive patterns. From that moment on, breaking the cycle became my mission.

This has been my journey, the path that has led me to where I am today. I have worked incredibly hard to build a life I love, and I am proud of what I have achieved. Most of all, I am proud that my children have grown into successful, happy individuals. Success, after all, is measured in happiness. That said, I know they have faced their own struggles. I tried my hardest, gave everything I could, but looking back, I realise that despite my best efforts, I probably only managed to give them half of what they truly needed. Not because I didn't love them, but because I was carrying the weight of my own abuse, and that is the tragedy of it.

Child abuse, or any abuse, affects children very badly. However, it affects the adults they become even more. It is a generational curse because, unfortunately, without intention, we repeat cycles without even realising it. I had stopped the cycle of child sexual abuse, but I had not stopped the cycle of my child's loneliness as the third daughter. My daughter spoke openly with me, and it made me sad because I had repeated a cycle—her loneliness, her feeling that I did not want her. In reality, she triggered my pain from my own lonely childhood, and she probably saw this fear as rejection. Luckily, we have a great relationship now. I reflected, changed, and made it right, once I knew. You cannot change the past, but by evolving into the best version of yourself, you can certainly change your future. We unconsciously continue repeating cycles, so we must start thinking outside our conscious mind. Otherwise, our reactions may unwittingly repeat the same patterns.

So, if you are reading this thinking, this happened to me, and there is still stuff going on, then the best thing to do is to tell someone.

Why am I telling you this? Well, firstly, when you have been abused, your processing is not the same as other people's, and this alone can make you feel abnormal. It is harder to take things in, to understand them, and you feel very insecure. That is completely normal. You are doing okay.

My memories of what happened to me are vague, not because I don't remember, but because I have blocked much of it out. Some moments stand out more than others, like my school days. I had friends, but I always preferred one-on-one interactions rather than being in a group. I struggled to trust people and felt anxious in large social settings.

Between the ages of four and nine, I used to play with dead rabbits. My parents even took photos of this. I remember my dad trying to bury one where I couldn't find it, but I always managed to dig it up again. This is a very strong memory—I can still see myself playing with them. I didn't understand that they were dead, but they were my friends. I am not quite sure why I played with them, and, to be honest, I wouldn't want this psychoanalysed. I will tell you something else too—now, I do not care what anyone, professional or otherwise, thinks of this behaviour. I am proud of it because it got me through a time that was barbaric and not normal. So, if my behaviour was not normal, so what? When I was younger, in my late teens and early twenties, it did bother me what people thought of me. I used to overthink things and always believe something was wrong with me. But there was nothing wrong with me, other than something very wrong happening to me.

So, if this resonates with you, then be reassured: it is not you!

Please accept my kind regards. Don't get me wrong, it has taken decades to think like this, and that is what I want to help with. This book is for all those in silent spaces, worried and feeling judged or abnormal.

You might find it helpful to break everything down into smaller, more manageable pieces and start seeing things in colour rather than just black and white. Focus on the people in your life who were involved in the conflict, consider how they may have helped or hindered you. Try putting yourself in their position and truly reflect on how difficult it may have been for them. This perspective can help you realise that it was never about you. A pervert could have chosen anyone. The fact that they chose you is not a reflection of who you are. You are pure and beautiful, that has never changed, and it never will. Being caught in that situation does not diminish your worth or perfection. It was not your fault.

You are special, and you were caught in a situation.

My mum knew about my grandad because she had been a victim herself. She truly believed that what happened to her was her burden alone and that he would never have harmed her children. Abuse distorts a person's internal functioning, and that is understandable, because the only person to blame is the perpetrator.

No one has the right to judge my mum, except those directly affected, and I choose to forgive her. She never failed me. She did her best with the abilities she had and within the circumstances she was forced into.

I invite you to walk with me through my journey. It is a privilege to share my story, and I find comfort in knowing you are here, turning these pages with me. My hope is that by sharing my experiences, lives will be saved, and the way we address child sexual abuse, or any form of abuse, will change.

My goal is for this subject to be discussed openly, without fear or judgement.

If someone confides in you, remember this: it is a true compliment of trust. Speaking out is terrifying, no matter one's age. That person has likely carried their secret for years. If we make them feel as though they are wrong for sharing, we only reinforce the stigma they have lived with.

And most importantly, they did nothing wrong. It was their life, their experience. Why should these stories be hidden? Why should we pretend this issue does not exist? The only way change will come is by speaking out.

With that said, please do not feel sorry for me. I have had a wonderful life, and my experiences have shaped me into the person I am today. My past allows me to help others, and I hope it contributes to changing the way we deal with child sexual abuse. I have chosen to write my entire life story to show the full scope of my journey, the highs, the lows, the joyful moments, the challenging times. Some of those challenges were a direct result of my abuse, but I want other survivors to know that it is okay to speak out. It is okay to share your story.

Don't get me wrong. The early years were difficult. Victims of abuse often struggle with self-hatred and have little to no self-esteem, it is completely understandable.

Chapter 2: Secrets Beneath the Surface

But things began to shift when I got a job at a petrol station during my final year of school. It helped me feel better about life. I worked with a boy named Cole. He was kind and polite, and after work, we would share a cigarette behind the garage in the supermarket car park. He let me ride his moped, and it was so much fun. It felt good to have a male friend who wanted nothing from me but friendship. Cole was tall and slim, and quite shy. In truth, I was shy too, until I got to know someone, and then I could be quite confident. We talked about all sorts of things, and I felt completely comfortable around him. We worked well together, and I actually looked forward to going to work when we were on the same shift. It felt more like a social event than a job. I was responsible for filling up petrol tanks, and my boss constantly reminded us not to go over the requested amount, as we would have to cover the difference. He would go on and on about how the petrol side of the business barely made a profit, and that the real money was in the shop. At fifteen, I didn't fully grasp the financial concern, after all, it was just petrol. I understood it to a degree, but did I really care? Probably not. Lucky for him, he couldn't read my mind. I earned just one pound an hour, with no extra pay for Sundays or bank holidays. But I wasn't working for the money, anyway.

During the week, I had to rush home to change after school as I started work at five o'clock till eight p.m. I worked Monday, Wednesday and Friday and Saturday twelve to six and Sunday ten till two, nineteen hours a week And yet I never felt tired, and I really enjoyed it.

Before I got the job, I used to ride a horse named April for the local coal man, Len. I loved it, though it did scare me a little. My dad didn't like me spending time with Len, and looking back, I can see why. An older man spending a lot of time with young girls, it could easily have been perceived as inappropriate. But in all honesty, Len never made me feel uncomfortable. He never did or said anything that made me uneasy. I think he simply enjoyed the company, and perhaps he knew young girls wouldn't gossip about his life.

Len lived in a terraced house, and stepping inside, it was immediately dark. The carpet had a well-worn path of trodden-in oil, likely from coal. The lounge was a mess, clothes draped over chairs, ashtrays overflowing, more ash beside them than inside. The carpet was thick with coal dust, and newspapers were scattered everywhere. Massive, old-fashioned armchairs surrounded a table in the centre of the room. The house itself was pre-war, with high ceilings. Despite the heavy smell of coal and smoke, there was an undeniable warmth, not just from the fire, but something deeper. A feeling of home, even in its messiness. Len was a tall, stocky man with thick, white hair. He always wore collared shirts under his overalls, though I never once saw him dressed up. His hair was swept back, probably

13

unwashed for days. His hands were rough and weathered, coal deeply embedded in his fingers and nails. He always wore sturdy boots, no matter the season. I enjoyed my time with him, and when my dad insisted I take the job at the petrol station, I was devastated. It meant I wouldn't see Len anymore.

My sister's friend had mentioned a job opening that she thought would be perfect for me. To be honest, I was terrified. I doubted my ability to do the job and feared what my dad would say if I wanted to quit. But deep down, I knew giving up wouldn't be an option. I had never been a confident person, largely because my mum used to call me 'thick'. She even referred to herself that way, as if it was something we had in common.

It never felt good to hear those words. My self-esteem was already low, and her comments only made it worse. There were times I wanted to cry, feeling small and insignificant. The thought of working in the garage filled me with dread. I worried that I wasn't capable and feared disappointing my parents if I failed.

Dad brought up the job one evening after I came home from spending time with Len. I didn't react enthusiastically, I simply said, "Oh, okay." Inside, I was disappointed. Taking the job meant giving up my chance to ride horses regularly, something I truly enjoyed. I also felt unprepared. I was only fifteen, and the job required me to be sixteen. But the boss didn't seem too concerned since my sixteenth birthday was approaching. That night, as I lay in bed, images of petrol pumps filled my mind. I kept wondering how I would manage to use them. The pressure of my dad's expectations weighed heavily on me. It was clear that I had no choice but to take the job, and quitting wasn't an option either. I asked my sister what the job entailed, but all she said was, "They'll teach you." That didn't help calm my nerves.

I started paying more attention to tills whenever I went into shops, worrying about whether I'd be able to operate one and give the correct change. My maths skills weren't great, and the thought of dealing with car parts at the garage overwhelmed me. How would I help a customer find the right lamp for their car when I knew nothing about such things? It all felt like too much. I had never been given much responsibility at home, especially in the kitchen, which made me overly reliant on others. Now, I was being thrown in at the deep end, with no way to back out. A couple of weeks passed without any mention of the job, and I started to feel relieved, hoping the opportunity had fallen through. Then, one day, my sister casually said, "Oh, I saw my friend today, she said the job starts a week on Monday, and it's yours if you want it."

Damn, I thought. Damn, damn, damn.

A funny feeling settled in my stomach. Even though I had loved riding April and spending time at Len's, something deep inside me knew I had to take the job.

That weekend, I went in to train with my sister's friend before officially starting. I was nervous when I arrived, but seeing Liz helped me relax. She was fun and easy going. I watched her refuel cars, and after observing for a while, she let me try. That's when Daniel, the boss, explained an important rule: I had to confirm the amount the customer requested before fuelling because some people would try to claim they had asked for less, forcing the garage to cover the difference. Surprisingly, the task wasn't as difficult as I had imagined. It even felt like a game, trying to stop the pump exactly on the amount requested. Of course, I went over a few times at first, and Daniel kept a close eye on me, reminding me that the garage ran at a loss on fuel. He was stricter than my dad, who constantly complained about leaving the lights on at home.

By the end of the day, I felt good about myself. It had all been much easier than I expected. I could now refuel cars and operate the till, at least the simple functions. Liz handled the more complicated tasks, but she assured me I had done really well, which meant a lot because I wasn't used to being praised. At the end of my shift, Daniel offered me a lift home in his Mercedes. He always made sure staff got home safely, especially after an incident where one of his female employees had been attacked while walking home in the dark. I think he was also more cautious because I was underage.

As I got into the car, I couldn't help but admire it. It felt luxurious, the seats were soft beige suede, the carpets were pristine, and the windows were automatic. Even at fifteen, I could appreciate how posh it was. My dad had always owned nice, new cars, but he had never had a Mercedes. Despite my admiration for the car, I was anxious about being alone in a confined space with a man. To distract myself, I focused on the car's features, trying to push away my unease. Thankfully, the ride was short, and I felt relieved as we pulled up to my house. I quickly got out, thanked him for the lift, and blurted out, "I really like your car!" I ran indoors with a chill down my spine, it was okay I reassured myself I am home, and he had not touched me, he was a good man. Although the evenings were not dark at the moment so I could see he was driving the right direction to home and that made me feel so much safer.

Once I was home, I ran straight to the kitchen, eager to see what was for dinner, I was starving.

"Stuffed hearts," my mum called out.

I grinned. I absolutely loved stuffed hearts. Not many fifteen-year-old girls would say that, but my mum could make almost anything taste amazing.

When I was younger, my mum used to cook rabbit quite often. Don't get me wrong, it tasted really nice but the tiny bones were awful. That was what put me off the dish, rather than the idea of eating rabbit itself. I suppose I never questioned it at the time because it had always been normal to me. As I got older, though, I didn't want to eat it anymore, and Mum eventually stopped offering it. Another dish I absolutely hated was liver and bacon, 'Yuck!' But to be fair, Mum was quite reasonable. She never forced me to eat things I truly disliked and would make me sausages instead. One of the best things about her was that she always cooked from scratch, and her food was always incredible.

I often went hungry during the day since I rarely ate breakfast and barely touched lunch, so by dinnertime, I was usually starving and would have eaten just about anything.

Mum had a rule: if you didn't eat, there was nothing else. We mostly accepted that. However, she never made us eat things she knew we genuinely hated. She learned that lesson the hard way after forcing my brother to eat something once, he projectile vomited everywhere. After that, she listened when we said we truly couldn't stomach something. But for the most part, we loved all her food.

As I sat down to enjoy my meal of hearts with boiled potatoes and vegetables, I smiled. Mum knew I loved hearts, and that small gesture made me feel loved. I picked up my knife and fork and started eating; it was delicious. At first, I had been a little disappointed to see boiled potatoes on my plate, but once I smashed them into the rich, homemade gravy Mum had made, they absorbed the sweet yet meaty flavour of the hearts. The gravy even made the vegetables more tolerable, though they were never my favourite.

The story behind my aversion to vegetables, however, was quite unfortunate. When I was about five or six, I once asked for seconds at school, not for pudding, but for more vegetables. A dinner lady took notice. My eyes had been bigger than my stomach, and I couldn't finish them all. Instead of letting me be, she forced me to eat every last bite. I ended up throwing up, and Mum had to come and collect me. She was not pleased, probably because she had been busy and was enjoying a moment of peace without me, but also because the dinner lady had essentially punished me for wanting more vegetables.

From that day onwards, I refused to eat them. I became scared that vegetables would make me sick again. Over time, Mum and I made compromises, I would happily eat raw carrots and peas, but cabbage was off the table. I hadn't liked gravy as a child, so she couldn't sneak vegetables past me that way either. But she understood. She knew I was a timid child, eager to please, and that I wouldn't refuse food without a real reason. So, she let me avoid certain vegetables, mainly cabbage, and for that, I was grateful.

After finishing dinner, I glanced at the clock; it was already nine o'clock. I decided to make myself a cup of tea and head to bed early since I had work the next day for more training. Earlier that evening, Liz had shown me how to read the meters on all the petrol pumps at closing time. She explained what to record and where to write it down. This would be my responsibility on Sunday, and surprisingly, I felt excited about it. The anxiety I had felt before was starting to fade, replaced by a sense of anticipation. As I lay in bed, I realised something important: actually, doing something you're afraid of is often easier than thinking about it beforehand. My mind always made things seem a hundred times harder than they actually were. Once I faced them, they were never as bad as I had imagined. There was a valuable lesson in this, but as I lay there, overthinking everything as usual, I knew I hadn't fully grasped it yet.

It was strange how, despite only being in training for a day, I already felt so much better about things. Oddly enough, this job felt right for me. I was even grateful to my dad for pushing me into taking it. Considering that I had given up the opportunity to go horse riding and have a horse of my own, it was surprising that I felt this was my path. I was no longer afraid. Instead, I felt excited about life. Having a job even made the idea of school more bearable. I had skived quite a bit, but now, knowing that I had work to look forward to, school didn't seem so bad. I could get through the school day knowing there was something worthwhile waiting for me. Note to self: Change, even when it seems scary, can actually improve your life.

Chapter 3: Whispers in the Dark

I had often skipped school. One time, I planned to do so with my cousin, who was a year younger than me. We had it all worked out. My sister, as usual, was willing to write me a sick note, as long as I did something for her in return, which I didn't mind. My cousin and I pooled our lunch money to buy cigarettes, ten John Player Specials, and some custard creams and bourbons. I wasn't big on sweets, but I did love biscuits, especially custard creams. That morning, we left for school as usual. To avoid suspicion, we signed in with our tutor group before slipping back out through the school gates. We had to be quick. Even though both of our parents worked, the thought of getting caught filled me with anxiety. My dad was strict, violently so. He had once beaten my brother nearly to death for skiving. I had witnessed it.

The memory came flooding back. I had been home from school that day when I overheard my dad telling my mum that Tim had hidden his bike behind the garage. His voice was tense with anger. I couldn't hear my mum's response, but I knew Dad was furious. Anxiety churned inside me as I heard him say, I'll sort him out. I did not know what he meant by that, but I knew he had a bad temper. I entered the kitchen and was then asked to leave, but I managed to briefly see into the garden.

I was worried about my brother. I wanted to warn him that Dad already knew he had skived school. I knew Tim would lie and say he had been, and the thought sent shivers down my spine. Dad was not good with lies. Lying meant punishment. Usually with the leather belt. I couldn't let Tim walk into this blindly. I tried to think of a way to warn him before he got home. But before I could come up with a plan, I heard the back door open. It was Tim.

I cringed as Dad's voice rang out immediately, sharp and furious. My heart pounded as I moved closer to the door, desperate to see what was happening. Dad had grabbed hold of Tim. I froze. Fear was written all over my brother's face, and it was an image that would never leave me. Then, Dad hit him. I backed away to the far end of the lounge, my whole body tense. Dad's voice had risen into a fit of rage, and before I knew it, he hurled Tim into the lounge wall. My stomach churned. I wanted to help, but I was paralysed by fear. Blood appeared on my brother's face as Dad kept punching him, over and over.

Mum screamed for him to stop, but he didn't listen. Instead, he threw her aside as if she were nothing.

I hated my father in that moment. I hated him for hurting my brother. I felt helpless, betrayed, and sick with anger. More than anything, I wanted Tim to know that I loved him.

After it was over, Tim retreated to his room. A while later, I approached Dad, asking for my pocket money early. He asked why, and I stuttered, saying I wanted to buy

Tim some sweets. He handed over the money, and I went to the shop. When I entered Tim's room, he barely looked at me.

"What do you want?" he muttered.

I handed him the sweets. "Here, these are for you."

He took them but didn't say anything. I could see the confusion and pain on his face. It mirrored my own feelings, feelings I had buried deep. The moment was unbearable, so I left without another word. I knew skiving was stupid, especially knowing what could happen if I got caught. But I hated school even more. Besides, it wasn't really my fault this time, it was my brother's lie that had set Dad off. At least, that's how I rationalised it. It was the only way I could cope with what had happened and still manage to look my father in the eye. Mum usually bore the brunt of Dad's fists. I hated it, but I had become used to it. As for my brother, he could write his own story if he wanted, though I doubted he ever would.

Well, Laura and I were off towards the manor farm, where the woods stretched behind it and a pond.

When we got there, we sat chatting and smoking. If I was honest, I never really liked smoking, but Dad did it, and my sister had been the one to get me started. I remembered the first time, she had taken the day off school, and I had skived with her. She even wrote me a note.

Hiding in the woods all day was surprisingly dull. I felt stuck, waiting for the inevitable question: Where had I been? It was different skiving with my sister. When she was around, the day felt shorter. We stayed indoors or went out together, and she always covered for me. She protected me, always had. Her motto was simple: If anyone could hurt me, it would be her, but no one else dared try. Much like any sibling.

As we sat by the pond, Laura looked straight at me and said, "You never told me what happened the day your secret came out."

Laura had always known my secret, she was my cousin and my confidant. I understood what she wanted to hear, but I had never spoken about that day out loud before. It had only just happened, and I wasn't sure I was ready to relive it.

My thoughts spiralled, tangled in uncertainty. Did I even want to open up about my trauma? It seemed like a simple decision, but it was far more complicated. That day, no one had reassured me, no one had held me. I had been left to process it all alone, cold and hollow. The only comfort I had received was my sister's embrace that evening, but even that felt distant now.

I took a deep, steady breath. The day everything unravelled, the day my secret was exposed, it was still vivid in my mind. The weight of it sat heavy on my chest. But I knew Laura was waiting, and maybe, just maybe, speaking the words would make them easier to bear.

So I began.

Chapter 4: The Day

Everything Changed

I was staying at my sister's house. She had recently married, and I loved spending time there. We were best friends, and I often stayed over. Our days were filled with laughter, music, and long chats. She always kept Pat's biscuits in the cupboard, and we would snack on them while listening to Lionel Richie, her favourite. In the evenings, when Pat came home from work, we would have dinner together, talking about everything and nothing. I always felt safe there. Pat was strong, protective, a presence that made me feel braver than I really was. That night, we decided to watch a thriller. I normally avoided scary movies, but with them, I felt like I could handle it.

The film was about a sorority house with a killer hiding in the attic, picking off the girls one by one. Black Christmas, I think that's what it was called. Pat had work the next morning, so he said goodnight and went to bed, leaving just my sister and me awake.

Out of nowhere, Suzanne my sister asked, "Do you have any secrets?"

I did. But I couldn't tell her.

I hesitated. "I have one, but I can't talk about it."

She didn't push. At least, not at first. We continued watching TV, but an hour later, she brought it up again.

"I don't like that you won't tell me. I'm your big sister. You should be able to tell me anything."

I was tired. My resistance was fading. The thought of upsetting her was unbearable, and exhaustion clouded my judgement. Without thinking, I muttered, "I can't tell you because of Mum."

Well, that was the end of my life as I knew it.

Everything was going to change.

I looked up at her and she said, "It's Grandad isn't it."

I didn't answer. I didn't have to. Tears spilled down her cheeks, and a mirror reaction swept over me. I felt the wetness on my face, the tightness in my throat, the snot clogging my nose. My sister's body shook with sobs.

"It's my fault. I should have told. If I had said something, it wouldn't have happened to you.

I'm so sorry, Mandy."

I looked at her, unsure if I had even responded with words. It was too much for me to comprehend. I didn't blame her, but I was confused, because all this time, I had thought I was alone in my terror. I had never thought it could be happening to her too. I felt numb. I couldn't absorb this new information. I felt suddenly scared like I had been caught being naughty. I felt vulnerable in the thought of my secret being found out. This was new territory, and I didn't like the uncertainty of it all.

Tears streamed down my face, whether from relief, grief, or sheer terror; I couldn't tell. It felt surreal. For so long, I had carried the weight of my secret in silence, yet here was my sister, saying it out loud. How did she know? The thoughts raced through me, paralysing me. My entire body tensed, every hair standing on end. I could only nod, as if betraying my secret without words, yet somehow, the truth was already spilling into the open.

My sister had her own experiences. She had pieced things together, and now she was confronting the terrifying possibility that what happened to her had happened to me too. In that moment, we were speechless, yet we kept going, both searching for closure, though neither of us truly understood what closure even meant. We embraced, clinging to each other. The warmth of that hug brought the first flicker of comfort in the midst of an unbearable truth. Somehow, in that moment, knowing we weren't alone eased the weight just a little. We spoke in hushed tones, exchanging fragments of our stories. One detail she shared was exactly what had happened to me.

Child sexual abuse had happened. Two girls, bound by trauma, finally breaking the silence. We had no idea how much horror would follow or how deep the wounds would run. So we did what we had always done: we tried to lock it away, to bury it, to pretend it wasn't real. Because that's what we knew. Silence.

But the fear lingered. Had I really told? The ramifications were unfathomable. This was not a good thing. I was exhausted, overwhelmed. We hugged tightly, seeking comfort in the only place it could be found. Eventually, we went to bed. I took the small front room, and she promised me that my secret was safe.

The next morning, I woke to a cold, damp sensation beneath me. I had wet the bed. Panic gripped me. This had never happened before. Shame flooded through me as I realised my nightdress and the sheets were soaked. How could I explain this? I had enough to deal with, how was I supposed to face my sister after last night? I needed to hide it. I peeled off the sheets, my mind racing for a solution. But before I could act, my sister walked in. I panicked, yanking the quilt over the wet patch. She sat down, right on it. I froze. As if the bedwetting wasn't bad enough, her next words shattered me completely.

"I promised to keep your secret," she mumbled, "but I told Pat. And he says we have to tell Mum and Dad." To say I hated her in that moment would be an understatement. The betrayal I felt was immediate, sharp, and all-consuming. I had only planned for a quiet evening at my sister's—something simple, something normal. Instead, in a single instant, my entire reality had been shattered. Everything I thought I knew about my life had been erased.

I barely registered her leaving the room. The wet bed didn't matter anymore. None of it did. Because now, the call was being made. I felt sick, blood draining from my body, nausea rising in my throat. But I couldn't cry. This was beyond tears. It was an emotion I had never felt before, one that words couldn't capture. Speaking my secret had made it real. For years, I had buried it so deep that, between visits, I could almost pretend it never happened. But now, it had been dragged into the light. And there was no way to hide from it anymore.

I could hear the clock ticking downstairs. Every time a car passed by, I tensed. Sitting on the bed, my body felt heavy, paralysed by the anticipation of what was coming. Then, the knock at the door. A single sound, but it carried the weight of a lifetime of fear.

I started to worry about getting into trouble because I had been convinced by my grandad that I wanted the sex. When he used to violate me as I reached my teenage years, I started to protest. He told me I was wet and I liked it. I didn't know what this meant, to be honest. I bit my lip to distract from the enormous internal pain and uncomfortableness and looked at him and stayed quiet with an insidious fear rising within me. I questioned why I had allowed him to do it. I questioned myself, I didn't like it but why had I not told? Why did I keep the secret? I waited until he had finished with me and we walked back home. He would tell me off for scuffing my feet.

That night, when my sister came into our shared bedroom, I asked her, "What does it mean when you're wet down there?" I pointed to my private parts.

She smiled and said, "It means you fancy a man."

I smiled back, but inside, something inside me shattered. If that was true, then what did that make me? The

29

guilt crushed me, suffocated me. I hated myself. More than anything, I hated myself. If my parents found out, they would hate me too. The thought made my stomach twist. I had to keep the secret. I had to.

Then, I heard voices downstairs. They started low, murmuring, but soon turned into whispers. Then, raised voices. My heartbeat pounded so hard it hurt. A wave of panic swept over me. My hands were shaking. My skin prickled. And then, I heard my name. It felt like a death sentence. I forced myself to move, dragging my heavy legs down the stairs. The carpet was soft beneath my feet, but it felt wrong. Like I was walking to my own execution.

In the living room, my father sat across from my sister. My mother was in the single-seater. As I entered, all three of them looked up at me. I hesitated, unsure where to sit. Finally, I perched on the edge of the two-seater, near my sister, close to the door, as far from my father as possible. Shame burned through me.

My father's voice was steady, but it cut through the air like a knife.

"Your sister tells me you have something to say."

I swallowed hard. My mouth was dry.

"She says your grandad touches you. Is this true?"

I stayed silent not sure what to say. He raised his voice and I nodded to try and stop him shouting. It didn't seem to work, he continued shouting.

"Are you sure?"

It Is Not How Life Starts, It Is How You

Finish It

"Are you sure?"

I sat there thinking. I didn't even want to tell, I was being made to, and now I'm being shouted at. My sister was there, why was dad asking me? why was I being punished? Did he think it was my fault?

Am I going to get into trouble?

My thoughts spun wildly, colliding with each other. I didn't know what he wanted me to say. If I had known, I would have said anything just to make him stop. Then, his voice erupted, shaking the room.

"Well, are you sure this happened?"

The fury inside me built up, but I didn't move. I turned to my mother, desperate for something, anything. She stood abruptly. Her voice was quiet, but firm.

"Of course, they're sure. They're not the only ones it happened to."

And with that, she fled the room, running up the stairs. I followed, relief washing over me because it meant I could leave too. In my sister's room, my mother collapsed onto the bed. She sobbed into the mattress, over and over, "It's my fault. It's all my fault."

At that moment, I held her close, reassuring her that none of it was her fault. I didn't fully grasp the significance of my words; I was simply trying to make my mother feel okay.

What I didn't realise then was that our roles were reversing. I was the child, yet I was the one offering comfort. I had no idea how this would shape me in the years to come. The weight of that simple act, giving my mother, my supposed caregiver, the reassurance I had always longed for.

Growing up, all I had ever wanted was for one of my parents to hold me and say, I'll protect you. I'll stop this. But that never happened. My mother's love had always felt distant, overshadowed by her shouting and the fear she instilled in me. Instead of love, I learned longing. The need for a cuddle ran so deep within me that it became something of an obsession. At night, I would imagine a man coming to rescue me. He would hold me, soothe me, comfort me. These hero stories played out in my mind as I fell asleep, my own way of finding warmth in a world devoid of affection. Even during the day, I found solace in my imaginary conversations. Riding my bike to school, I would talk to myself, lost in my own world.

My friend often caught me. "I saw you talking to yourself again," she would tease. I'd smile, laugh it off, and deny it. She never meant any harm, she was a close friend, someone I trusted. But she was right. I was talking to myself. And the truth was, I didn't mind being caught. It never stopped me from doing it.

Once the secret was revealed, and my mum had finally detonated the grenade of truth, exposing, for the first time, her own childhood horrors to my father, our house descended into a bleak silence. The next day, they carried on as if nothing had happened. No one asked me what had happened. No one asked if I needed help. No one held me.

No one spoke to me about it ever again. I was left alone with my fear, confusion, and pain, drowning in sorrow and still questioning whether I was to blame.

My father had always been a good dad, or at least, in his mind, he had tried to keep us safe. But it was confusing. Here was my daddy, the man who worked hard, showed me kindness, and provided for my needs. Yet, as a husband, he was different, chauvinistic, controlling. If my mum dared to challenge him, there would be trouble. It was a common occurrence: coming home from school to a silent house, then hearing their raised voices, mum running past me, dad chasing after her, fists flying. I would sit, pretending to be engrossed in the television, hoping to remain invisible.

Life in that house was suffocating. Silence weighed heavier than the violence. I was rarely allowed outside, unlike my siblings, who had so much more freedom. Being the youngest, I was kept close, too close. But I never felt wanted. Sitting alone in my room was isolating, but it was still better than sitting with them.

I thought about all of this as I told my story to Laura. She sat in silence, listening, not interrupting even once. She knew my father well, he was her uncle. She feared him too, even though he had never raised his voice at her. It was his presence, his unspoken command to behave... or else. She had heard my stories of his violence, of me running to her house just to escape the storm.

After I finished, we took a walk, trying to shake off the weight of it all. I could see the guilt on Laura's face, guilt for bringing back my memories. She needed relief as much as I did. Laura had timed our walk back to school perfectly, deciding that we should wait in the Esso Cinema car park until we could hear the school bell. That way, we could blend in with the other students walking home, making it seem as though we had been in school all along. When we arrived at the cinema, it was unexpectedly busy. A sudden wave of uncertainty washed over me.

I said, "Let's wait under the building a bit so we cannot be seen."

My heart was pounding now, fear creeping in at the thought of getting caught. Dad could be violent; I had seen it too many times with Mum and had watched him beat Tim for skiving. Even though he had only given me the belt once and had never laid a hand on me otherwise, I was still afraid of him. Maybe it was his constant shouting or his unpredictability, but the fear was always there.

Trying to appear indifferent, I stood there waiting for the bell. I turned to Laura, voicing my concern. "Do you think the bell has already gone?"

She shook her head. "I don't think so," she said, then added, "I'll go and check."

She stopped suddenly, turned around and said, "Oh my God, Mandy, your dad is here."

At first, I thought she was joking which to be fair would have been something I myself would do but as I turned to look, I could see him from our car coming towards us. I didn't have the courage to look at his face and I didn't know what to do. Laura said, "What shall we do?"

I swallowed hard and my hands seemed to go to an instant sweat, well there was only one thing to do right now and that was to walk to the car and wait to see his reaction.

I knew not to lie!

Truth was rewarded normally!

But fear gripped me as we approached. I envied Laura; she was safe. No matter what happened, her mum would blame me for leading her astray. That was always the story, I was the bad influence, the troublemaker. In reality, we had both been just as bad as each other, pushing boundaries together. But my upbringing had been harsher, rougher. Maybe I did take the lead in mischief. The car door opened. Dad's voice rang out, but something was off. His tone wasn't what I expected. He sounded… calm.

"What we had been doing?" he asked.

"We just walked here, chatting. We were going to come home soon," we replied casually.

Was that a lie? We hadn't said we had been to school? I got in the car, still unsure whether his mood would change. I was so scared of him dropping off Laura! knowing that as long as Laura was with us, he wouldn't say anything. He never did in front of others. When we arrived at her house, my hands grew clammy again, and a strange thumping sensation pulsed in my head, not quite a headache, but something close. The rest of the drive home was silent. He said nothing, which in some ways was worse. The waiting, the uncertainty, not knowing if his anger was still coming. When we got home, he remained quiet. I did the same, too afraid to say anything. The silence stretched through the evening, suffocating me. I hated my life. I felt utterly alone, but I clung to the thought that my new job might change that.

After that day, life carried on as if nothing had happened. I went to school, and no one spoke to me about my past. It was as though I had revealed everything, been met with anger and doubt, had my mother confirm it, and then... nothing. Just like that. I couldn't wrap my head around it. Loneliness settled in deep. My siblings had their own lives, and I had no one to confide in. I had never liked school much, but something had changed. I had started to develop an attitude that made me more noticeable and that gained me friends. For the first time in a long time, school felt good. It became my escape, a haven where I could breathe. I didn't see it as a place to learn; how could I, when my mother had called me thick for as long as I could remember? She never meant it to be cruel, at least I don't think she did. But it didn't feel nice either. She thought she was thick herself and, in some twisted way, seemed to want company in that belief.

For the first time in all my years at school, I had begun to feel safe. I particularly enjoyed my typing class because I had many friends there. We would sneak cigarettes in the toilets during lessons, acting out and pushing boundaries. My friends seemed to enjoy my rebellious nature, and I thrived on their approval, it was something I rarely received at home. Even before I entered the classroom, the teacher would blame me for any disruption. Sometimes, she even locked me in another teacher's room, though he would eventually let me out. Back then, teachers were allowed to hit students and throw things at them. Yet, in the beginning, this same teacher had told me I was naturally talented at typing and that I could get a good job if I pursued it. That small bit of praise had made me feel good about myself, and she even put me forward for a Pitman typing exam. I passed the first one. But when I failed the next exam, the disappointment hit me hard. It confirmed what I had always been told at home, that I was a failure. My self-esteem crumbled, and instead of trying again, I gave up. It was easier to act out in class, to be the funny one, the naughty one, the one who made people laugh. That way, I could feel liked, even if only temporarily. But deep down, I knew these friendships were surface-level. The girls in my group would say hello in the playground, but it never felt real. I had always preferred having just one close friend; it felt safer that way.

School had always been difficult for me because I was terrified of being noticed. As a child who longed to fade into the background, to become invisible and hide my vulnerability, school was a place I dreaded. I never knew which adults I could trust. If I couldn't trust my grandad, then who could I trust? That thought haunted me, though at the time, it lingered more as an unprocessed feeling rather than a conscious realisation. Mixed messages had shaped my life, leaving me confused and unsure. I had learned not to ask questions, doing so would only provoke my mother's anger. She would scream and shut me down, making me feel as if I were a nuisance for simply wanting to understand things. My father became my go-to instead, though even that was limited. Deep down, I felt my mother hated me. I rarely felt love from her, and so, I avoided communication with her at all costs.

That insecurity at home only made school feel even more frightening. My siblings teased me constantly, and when they babysat me while my parents were out, I often ended up in casualty. But instead of concern, I was made to feel as if I was the problem, just a troublesome child who caused inconvenience.

My earliest school memories were filled with fear. I would sit at the back of the class, desperate to be good but too anxious to focus. My mind was constantly clouded with confusion and fear, making it impossible to engage in lessons such as openly express any real questions I had because of this residing fear in within me.

There were moments when I enjoyed learning, though—especially my times tables. I loved practising them at home because I liked knowing the answers. But that joy disappeared when the teacher called on me to recite them in front of the class. Standing on my chair, answering questions, was humiliating. I was terrified of making a mistake, of being teased. Those moments made me doubt myself even more.

Chapter 5: Breaking the Cycle

Now, with my new job at the garage, I finally felt a sense of stability. At first, I had been hesitant about the job, but it was turning out to be a source of comfort, a small, solid piece of my life when everything else felt so uncertain.

That morning, I had woken up later than usual. It was already nine o'clock, and I had to be at work by ten. Now, I felt rushed. I had wanted to take my time getting ready, to ease into the day, but instead, I had to quickly pick an outfit, shower, and walk to work. The walk only took fifteen minutes, but with just forty-five minutes left and my eyes barely open, I knew I had to hurry. I dragged myself out of bed and rushed to the bathroom for a shower. After drying off, I tossed my towels on the floor and rummaged through my clothes. Jeans and a top would do, I had practically lived in jeans for years. I pulled on my big, baggy jumper with black and beige stripes. My sister had bought it for me, and it meant the world to me. It made me feel loved, and I particularly liked how it covered my bum. I often visited my eldest sister, where we'd sit together, drinking tea and eating biscuits. Thinking of that made me smile, but I had no time to dwell on it. I slipped on my trainers and wondered what the day would bring. The odd thing was, even though I had been eager to get back to work the night before, I suddenly felt nervous again. I tried to push the feeling aside.

In the kitchen, Mum was already up. She asked how I was feeling, but I just grunted, grabbed my toast, and rushed out the door.

"See you tonight! What's for dinner?" I called over my shoulder.

"Sunday roast, of course!" she shouted back.

"Oh, right! I forgot it was Sunday." Since I had worked the previous day, the weekend had flown by, and I liked that. I loved a Sunday roast, so at least I had that to look forward to when I got home. Besides, I was only working until two today. As I walked up the road, I let my mind wander, slipping into my usual daydreams. I often imagined someone rescuing me, it was a thought that helped me fall asleep at night. Sometimes, though, I got so lost in my thoughts that I would catch myself mumbling out loud in public. I saw the supermarket up ahead and, in an instant, my anxiety faded. I picked up my pace, eager to get to work. I've already done one shift, how bad can today be? As I walked into the forecourt, a sense of belonging washed over me. I spotted Liz behind the till, laughing as usual. She was always so cheerful, and it was nice to be around her.

"Hiya!" she called, waving me over.

There was a customer at the till, and Liz grinned. "Mandy can serve you."

I swallowed my nerves, ready to practice. What could possibly go wrong with Liz watching over me?

The man had bought cigarettes and petrol, which came to twelve pounds. He handed me fifteen, and I gave him his three pounds change.

"You should've offered him a receipt," Liz reminded me.

"Oh, sorry," I said quickly.

"No worries, I don't need one," the man replied with a smile.

I made a mental note to remember next time. Liz then opened the till and showed me how to process receipts and handle other types of transactions, including those for garage parts and labour. At the back of the shop was a mechanic's area, and part of the store sold car parts. That section seemed complicated, with everything listed in a catalogue. Just as I was trying to get my head around it, a man came in asking for a bulb.

"Just give me the catalogue, and I'll tell you the number to look for," he said.

I found the bulbs easily once he gave me the number. Simple! I was relieved he knew what to do because, at that moment, Liz had gone upstairs to see Daniel, leaving me alone. But I had managed, and that made me feel really good about myself.

Later, Liz took me upstairs to introduce me to Denise, who worked in accounts. Denise's office was in a cosy little back room near Daniel's office. I stood quietly while Liz chatted away, but after a while, I started wondering who was looking after the shop.

I asked Liz, "Should I go back to the shop?"

Liz assured me, "You're okay, Daniel is down there at the moment making a cuppa, but when he comes back, we will go back down and make ourselves a drink."

Once we went downstairs and made a drink, Liz showed me how to set up a tab. She explained that we could help ourselves to anything in the shop as long as we noted it on the tab, which would then be deducted from our weekly pay. This felt really good, she whispered. Of course, we often forget to put things on the tab, don't we?

I smiled, unsure if this was a trick question.

We went back into the shop and she took a chocolate bar and threw one at me and said, "Come on, let's have a break and drink our tea." I felt really relaxed although I couldn't help thinking about the Daniel coming in and asking about the chocolate, and as I thought this, he suddenly appeared behind us and asked, "Are they on your tab Liz?" She just laughed and he walked back upstairs nonplussed.

I was starting to feel really relaxed and when I checked the time, I realised we only had an hour left and I asked, "Do you want me to mop the floor?" I had done that in the previous night and Liz said, "Yes, that is a good idea." She then added, "Is it that time already."

I asked, "Is it too early?" and she replied, "No carry on, it needs doing, and we need to get everything ready to close. I don't expect anyone will be in now for parts anyway."

The parts shop had a different till and was on the opposite area of the station, though it shared the same entrance. It was possible for someone to be there without you realising.

After I finished mopping the floor, Liz said, "Oh, I haven't shown you the diesel pump out the back yet because we haven't had any trucks or lorries in, but you'll need to know how to use it."

She explained that during the week, we'd likely have one or two trucks needing diesel, and I'd need to handle the pump. It worked the same way as the petrol pumps, but drivers used gloves because diesel was messier. She also showed me how to unlock and lock the pump each time, as it was out back where someone could use it without us knowing. Then, she pointed out the key's location and explained how to take a reading. A sudden wave of anxiety hit me. What if I couldn't find the key? What if I messed up the reading? I had a habit of doubting myself, and this was no different.

Next, it was time for me to read the pumps at the front forecourt. I tried to remember what Liz had taught me the night before. Nervous but determined, I grabbed the clipboard, pen, and record sheet before heading to pumps one through four in order. At least I had done that part right.

Liz smiled. "Well done."

43

I was pleased with myself, more pleased than she was, to be honest. A warm, satisfying feeling spread through me.

She said, "You can go home now."

I felt a little sad as I had enjoyed my day.

"Daniel is pleased with you," Liz added. "He will see you tomorrow at five, don't be late. Oh, and you will be working with Cole."

A pang of nervousness hit me. Liz wouldn't be there tomorrow, and I worried whether I would be able to do the job without her guidance. After saying my goodbyes, I started walking home, passing the supermarket, which was closed since it was Sunday. The streets were empty, but as I walked, I thought about the roast dinner waiting for me at home. The thought made my steps quicker. When I arrived, the familiar smell of my mum's cooking filled the air. I walked into the kitchen and saw my dinner had been left in the oven.

I called out, "Is this dinner for me?"

"Yes," Mum replied. "You might need to put it in the microwave."

I didn't bother. I was too hungry. The plate was piled with chicken, runner beans, cabbage, peas, roast potatoes, and gravy. I had recently started liking gravy more, it helped disguise the taste of cabbage. After dinner, I called Laura to see if she was busy and went over to her house. We didn't see each other as much anymore since school had taken us in different directions, but weekends were still ours to catch up. Would that change now that I had a job? I wasn't sure, but for now, we had time.

Aunty Pat was out, so we had the house to ourselves. We played music and danced around like teenagers do, then decided to go for a walk. We walked halfway to my house before saying our goodbyes since we both had school in the morning.

"I'll tell you all about meeting Cole," I promised her. Secretly, I hoped he was handsome and that I'd fall madly and deeply in love with him.

We lit a cigarette and slipped into the close to smoke, making sure we wouldn't get caught. After finishing, we started walking towards my house. When we reached the halfway point, I left Laura and continued the rest of the journey alone. Back to my daydreams. Back to the conversations in my head that felt so real, until I caught myself again, noticing the strange looks from passers-by. Oops, I thought. Though, to be honest, I didn't really care what strangers thought. It was only embarrassing when my school friends caught me at it. I hurried past them, pushing the thoughts back into my head, trying to keep my mouth from betraying me again. I looked up and realised I was nearly home. You see, when I dreamed, time flew by, and everything seemed easier. The dreams helped me more than anything else, and I had no desire to give them up. They were my little secret, these imagined conversations where I had complete control, where bad things didn't happen. I stepped inside and hesitated, wondering what to do next. Tomorrow couldn't come soon enough. Now that I had gotten myself all excited about Cole, the anticipation was almost unbearable. Maybe I'd make a cuppa and take it to bed with a book. Before long, it would be time to sleep anyway.

I had overslept the next morning, and my heart was racing. You might wonder why I was worried about being late when I usually skived off school and had a bad attitude. But in truth, this wasn't my natural character. I had anxiety, I couldn't bear being the last one to walk into class with everyone turning to look at me. Just the thought of it made me feel sick. I threw my clothes on, not even bothering to wash, and rushed out the front door. I didn't usually eat breakfast anyway, though I did at least wash most mornings. Catching up with some friends on the way helped me relax slightly, until I remembered we had cooking that day, and I had forgotten my ingredients. There was no time to go back now. I'd just have to get into trouble. Mrs Reynalds, our cooking teacher, was kind. She would probably say, help me cook mine if you like. But even then, I would feel awkward about it. And then it hit me, I hadn't packed my PE kit either. Miss Cox, on the other hand, was not so nice. She would make me tuck my skirt into my knickers. Just what I need when my day has already started horribly!

As if that wasn't enough, I suddenly remembered I was working at five. This is not going to end well, I thought. I'm going to meet Cole while I'm all sweaty because there won't be time for a shower after school. There was only an hour and ten minutes between school and work, and I was never very organised. I often avoided asking my mum for things because I didn't fancy being shouted at for looking for my cooking ingredients or needing my PE kit washed.

It Is Not How Life Starts, It Is How You Finish It

The day had started off terribly.

When I arrived at school, I was greeted by a bunch of girls who seemed eager to say hello. I always felt like an imposter. Everyone seemed to think I was cool, yet I was the most uncool person in school. Well, not the most uncool, there were some real geeks, but I definitely didn't fit in. Still, I continued chatting regardless. I had learnt early on how to put on a front in the face of adversity. I never really liked school, mainly because of my bad experiences in primary school. One particular memory haunted me. I used to poo my pants.

Even now, I could vividly recall one day when I was sitting in class, and every time I moved my bum cheek, I could smell it. I was desperately hoping the bell would ring soon to end the lesson. My mind was so consumed with panic that I could barely hear what the teacher was saying. Fear ran through me, what if someone noticed? Andrew was sitting closer to me today than usual. He often sat with me, but he had never mentioned anything before. Still, I always wondered if he could smell it. Surely, he could. I anxiously glanced around at the others sitting near me, searching for any sign of reaction. The thought of being exposed was unbearable. I didn't know how I would handle it if someone spoke up. Then my mind raced ahead to how I was going to get rid of the mess when I got home. I decided I would take off my pants and flush them down the toilet. But that might cause another blocked toilet, which was already becoming a common problem in our house. Mum would then threaten to take me to the doctor, convinced that something was wrong with me. The smell was getting worse.

I often asked myself why I didn't just raise my hand and ask to go to the toilet like any other child. But for some reason, I couldn't. It always started with the thought that I needed to go, then the hesitation to put my hand up, and suddenly, it was too late. I didn't understand why it happened. The memory faded, and I was brought back to the present.

I had PE next.

I casually tried to mention to my friends that I didn't have my kit, testing the waters to see their reaction. That was a mistake. Their reactions were no what I needed to hear. "OMG, Miss will kill you!" one of them said, the other one laughed and said, "Guess who will be tucking her skirt in her knickers!" I forced a smile as if I could handle the micky take, but in truth, I felt like crying.

Walking into the classroom, I felt even worse. There was another class joining us today, full of students I had never seen before. My world had just gotten even worse. I felt too shy to tell the teacher in front of all these new people. But my so-called friend didn't hesitate.

"Miss Mandy has not got her kit!" she blurted out, laughing.

About six or seven others joined in, laughing. I blanked it out and forced a laugh, pretending not to care. That only made things worse, now I looked like I didn't take it seriously. To my shock, Miss Cox simply said, "Just get out of my class and report to your tutor. Tell them you have nothing to do."

The shame was unbearable. This was beyond embarrassing. But strangely, I was relieved to be out of that room. I wondered if my friends would even talk to me after this. My tutor was actually quite nice about it. He said, "If you have any work to catch up on, then do it now." I had loads of homework due in this week which I never done at home. This felt like a little win because Mr Fletchers English homework was due in next class, so I sort of felt saved from that fate.

I wanted this day to be over, but I also wasn't looking forward to work. When the bell rang, my tutor dismissed me. I gathered my things and hurried off. I had further to walk than the others, and I didn't want to be late for class, especially since I now believed no one liked me anyway. At least I had managed to finish my homework. Well, whether I had done it correctly was another matter. I didn't pay much attention in class, especially when teachers explained the homework. My mind always wandered, usually daydreaming about being rescued by Cole. He was handsome, kind, and gentle. I had almost forgotten that I probably smelled. Although, if I had been made to do PE, it would have been much worse. At least something good had come out of this day. But I definitely didn't want a repeat of it.

The classroom was already half full when I arrived, and I quietly slipped into my usual seat. To my surprise, my mates came over, patting me on the back and sitting down beside me like I was some sort of brilliant gangster. If only they knew the truth. If only they knew I was faking it all, that deep down, I had wanted to cry and run out of school, never to come back. But they didn't know, because the whole thing was just a façade.

Truth is, I never liked that much attention. I didn't want to be a hero, and I definitely didn't want to be a laughingstock either. I just wanted, more than anything, not to be noticed at all. Then the bell rang. The best bell of the whole day. Home time.

My friends were all planning to meet behind the cinema for a cigarette, but I had to rush home. At first, I thought I could join them for a few minutes, just a quick chat, then head off. After all, the cinema was next door. But that plan quickly unravelled. We ended up waiting around for everyone to show up, and time was slipping away. I told them I had to leave because of my new job. "You didn't tell us!" they shouted. Exactly, I hadn't wanted them turning up at my workplace and getting me sacked. My dad would kill me if that happened.

I couldn't bring myself to care anymore. I had detached from them emotionally. Now, I was just feeling anxious about meeting Cole and starting the job, especially since I wasn't confident about what I was doing yet. Back inside my head, I drifted into a daydream, imagining Cole looking into my eyes and smiling, walking towards me and saying, "Don't worry, I'll show you the ropes." Surprisingly, I got home quicker than expected and even had time for a cuppa. I filled the kettle, set it to boil, and just sat there, reeling from a day I thought would never end. But here I was, sitting quietly in the kitchen, savouring a moment of calm. Life, just for now, felt okay, and I was relishing it. Cole could wait. Right now, all I wanted was this small moment to myself. As the kettle boiled, Mum came through and said, "Yes, please, I'll have one of those."

I looked up at the clock and said, "I've got work and I only boiled enough for one." She replied, "That's all I want, just one."

I laughed and said, "You can make it, then," and walked off before she could clip me round the ear. Not that she ever did; Mum wasn't one for hitting. She just shouted. A lot.

I pulled on my jeans and sprayed deodorant over my unwashed skin, thinking it was better than nothing. Then it hit me: my mum had put the T-shirt I was planning to wear in the wash. I felt devastated. If I'd had that top, I would've felt more relaxed and more confident. Now I had to find something else to wear, something that wouldn't make me look three sizes bigger. I felt cross and frustrated and shouted, "Where are my tops?"

She shouted back, "Probably on the floor where you leave all the clean washing I put in your room!"

I looked down, and sure enough, a red top was poking out from under the pile of clothes, the very same pile I'd chucked on the floor in my mad rush to school that morning.

I bent down to grab it and thought, Crap, I'm going to be late again. And once again, I felt like crying. Honestly, how many times in one day can a person feel like crying? I sound like some kind of cry-baby. Actually, my family did tease me about that growing up. Maybe they were right.

I rushed to find my shoes; luckily, they were by my bedroom door, which was a miracle in itself and bolted outside, tying them as I went.

Mum shouted, "You've got pork chops for dinner!"

That made me smile, and I scooted off faster than usual.

By the time I reached the top of our road, I'd calmed down a bit. I still had fifteen minutes to get to work, and the full journey only took that long; plus, I'd already covered part of it.

I slowed my pace and, predictably, started thinking about Cole, my imaginary, handsome hero, the one who'd sweep me off my feet and rescue me from this life. If only I'd understood the weight of that feeling back then, maybe I could've avoided a few of the potholes that were waiting for me later on.

I could see the supermarket ahead, which meant I was nearly there and about to find out what Cole was really like. As I turned the corner, I noticed a slim boy standing by the till, smiling at me. It felt strange. He was nothing like I had imagined and not at all my usual type. But there was something about his demeanour that immediately put me at ease. He looked friendly, and that was all I really needed right now. I still wasn't confident in my role, and the idea of working with someone approachable felt like a relief. He didn't match the image I'd built in my head; he certainly didn't look like the "rescuer" type. Tall and slim, not exactly handsome but not unattractive either. Just... ordinary. Still, the moment I saw him, I had a sense that we were going to get on just fine.

I walked straight up to him and held out my hand to say hello. He looked at me, laughed, and said, "Chill out." I quickly dropped my hand, trying to downplay my eagerness.

He didn't make a big deal out of it, thankfully. Instead, he said, "I hear you did a really good job over the weekend. Don't worry, I'll help you out with anything you're not sure on as long as you mop the floor at night."

I hoped he was joking, but honestly, I didn't mind mopping every night if that's what it took. Still, something about the way he said it made me think he'd never actually make me do it. He was the perfect gentleman.

Daniel wasn't there; it was just Cole and me. As soon as I arrived, he offered me a cuppa.

"Today I make the tea," he said. "Friday's your turn."

I nodded, wondering if he really meant it, and smiled as he walked past me. Just then, I noticed someone walking towards the shop; they probably needed fuel. My stomach twisted with nerves, and I felt slightly sick. But I also knew I could do it. Should I wait for Cole or take initiative? What could really go wrong?

I stepped forward and said, "Hello, how can I help you?"

"Ten pounds, please," he replied.

"Right," I said, confirming, "That was ten pounds, yes?"

He nodded, and for a second, I wasn't sure if I should say anything else. I hoped I didn't have to repeat myself; I was too shy for that. I put in exactly ten pounds, and he handed me the cash without a fuss. I have to admit, I felt a little proud of myself. As I walked back into the shop, I couldn't help but give a small wiggle of my hips, feeling, for a moment, like I'd nailed it. I hoped Cole was still out the back. But unfortunately, he wasn't. He was standing there, blushing slightly, giving me a shy, coy smile. Surprisingly, Cole seemed even more shy than I was, which, in a strange way, worked entirely in my favour.

Cole certainly made me feel like part of the team. True to his word, he had made all the teas. I thought to myself, I'll have to make up for this on Friday, and smiled; strangely, I didn't really care. I had never had a boy as a friend before. I usually kept my distance from boys, but Cole was different. In many ways, he felt more like a girl. Don't get me wrong, he looked completely like a boy, but he had a heart of gold. Pure gold. I sensed it the moment I saw his face. If life had taught me anything in my younger years, it was that I needed to read people quickly if I was going to survive.

One day flowed into the next, and I found myself genuinely enjoying my job at the garage. I was so pleased with my dad's choice; it turned out to be one of the best things that had happened to me in a while. As soon as the school bell rang, I'd rush home, excited to get to work. It felt like having a social life again. I was getting to know the regular customers, and it gave me a sense of purpose. The only time I felt nervous was when someone needed a part for their car. Thankfully, most of them looked it up in the book themselves. Perhaps they saw the blank expression on my face and thought, Just give me the book, not wanting to risk paying for the wrong part.

After about a month, I started getting waved at by this guy who always came in with a friend. He never drove; he always sat in the passenger seat. I felt a bit awkward once I started to recognise them. Somehow, knowing who they were made it feel like more pressure. It was as if I were being watched, and that made me uncomfortable. They were around my age, give or take a year or two. Probably in either my brother's year or my sister's, not the eldest one, but the sister who was two years older than me, or maybe my brother's year, who was three years above.

Anyway, they only came in about once a week, sometimes less. I was starting to get a bit of attention at work, and I noticed people looking when they came in. But unfortunately, I hadn't liked any of them. I was still heartbroken over my first boyfriend. We'd broken up six months ago, but it still lingered in me like a bruise that never quite healed.

It was my last year at school, and I had no idea what I wanted to do next. Dad said I should go full-time in the garage, but when I asked about college, Mum said, "You're thick, so you're better off working in the garage full-time."

Even though I had hated school, my sister had gone to college, and no one was even offering it to me. It reminded me of my French lessons. I'd been told I couldn't take French because my English wasn't good enough. Instead, I had to use the time to catch up on English and try to improve my grades.

Not being allowed to take French was the final straw. I gave up trying in class after that. I remember thinking, school can stuff it up their bum. It made me feel sad and humiliated. I'd looked forward to learning French, especially because we had French students at school and, truth be told, I fancied one of them. So to be told I wasn't allowed to learn it made me furious and deeply disappointed. I wanted my mum to complain, to stick up for me, but I didn't even ask her. I was too afraid. Deep down, I knew what she'd say, that I was too thick to do it anyway. What was the point? I had no say in it. So I just accepted it or rather, stopped caring. I was so disheartened that I became naughty in class from that day on. I felt completely let down. It seemed so unfair. All my friends were allowed to do it, and I wasn't. It made me feel even more like an outsider. Oddly, none of them teased me about it. Maybe they noticed how upset I was. I don't know. But at least that was something, one small mercy in it all.

That was how I came to be labelled as 'naughty'. And now, with school nearly behind me, came another blow, this time from my parents. I was told I wouldn't be allowed to go to college. My self-esteem took a real hit. In truth, I didn't think much about it at all because it hurt too much. Instead, I buried the feelings and kept going, continuing to work at the garage. Then summer arrived, and school was finally over. But it didn't feel as satisfying as I'd imagined. I had finished school in May, though not in the usual way. I hadn't taken my exams—not properly, anyway. I only turned up for two: Needlecraft and Religious Studies. Despite everything, I still believed in God. Even though my life often felt harder than a piece of overcooked meat left to rot in the garden for a week, I believed He was there, beside me. I couldn't explain it, but I felt His presence, even in the darkest times.

I had a life now. Things had changed. I seemed to be getting invited out much more, and I was always busy. With school over, my days felt freer, and I often just offered to help out at the garage.

One evening, I was invited to a barbecue. I didn't really want to go, but I forced myself to make the effort. I pulled on my favourite jeans and jumper and headed out to my friend's place. It was going to be full of people from my group, my "yes group" friends, and that was part of why I wasn't completely sure I wanted to go.

Still, I'd made the effort. I walked steadily down the road, and it looked like it might rain. That worried me because I hadn't brought a coat. But it was June; why would I even think to wear one? It had already rained earlier, and the road was lined with massive puddles. As I walked towards one of them, I noticed a car coming in the opposite direction. I timed it in my head and realised they might hit the puddle just as I passed. And they did. Five boys inside the car cheered as they steered directly into the water, drenching me from head to toe. I could feel my jeans clinging to my skin, my pants soaked through. I'd washed my hair earlier and now looked like a drowned rat. I was mortified and furious at once, especially because they were boys from my peer group, boys who looked cool.

I turned around and decided to go home. Then, as I walked, another car drove past and beeped. I saw a hand wave out the window, but I didn't recognise the car or the person. I assumed they were teasing me too, laughing at my misfortune. Even though it was June, I felt cold, the dampness soaking into me. I had nothing else to wear. I couldn't go now. I'd told my friends I was coming, and I hated the idea of letting them down. When I got home, I sulked. I ran a bath, feeling fed up and flat. Mum asked why I was back, and I told her what happened. She said, "I've just put some more clothes on your bed—why don't you get changed and go?"

But I didn't want to bother anymore. It's not like I was looking forward to it in the first place. As I lay in the bath, I started to notice my body shape. I felt uncomfortable. The jeans I'd had on were comfy, but the other pair, the ones on the bed, rode up into my crotch and were tighter. I was on my period too, which always made me feel bloated. And hungry, I'd eat anything in sight when I was like that.

I was looking forward to eating the barbecue for that reason. The period had probably not helped my state of mind.

Something strange happened; I suddenly felt the urge to go to the party after all. I had already told my friends I was going, and if I didn't show up, they'd probably be annoyed with me. So, I pulled on my uncomfortable jeans, thinking maybe they'd loosen up after a while. I did my usual trick, crouching down and bouncing a few times to try and stretch them out. They were always a bit better after a day's wear since they had some give in them. Trying to ignore the tightness around the seams, I threw on a different top and decided I was ready to give the evening another go.

I had decided that next time I'd be more careful; I would watch out for cars and stop before reaching the puddle. But strangely, when I walked down the same road again, the sun was beating down and the puddle had almost vanished. It felt like I had stepped into a different reality.

Fortunately, I hadn't put on another jumper, and to my surprise, my top, a summer one, was just right for the weather. As I walked, I saw the same car coming towards me again. The one with the person who had waved. They hadn't splashed me, only laughed, but I still felt embarrassed knowing they'd seen me at my lowest. The car slowed this time and the window was down. It turned out to be one of our regular customers from the garage. He gave a massive smile, waved, and beeped again. My embarrassment lingered, but now it was for a different reason. I wasn't used to this kind of attention, and I didn't like being noticed.

When I arrived at the barbecue, I felt horrible. Everyone had already eaten, and I was far too shy to ask for food. I was starving, and I could see the food laid out, but I just didn't have the confidence to leave my friend's side and go help myself. When they encouraged me to get something, I lied and said I'd already had dinner, though my stomach hated me for that. Mum hadn't cooked for me either, since I'd told her I'd be eating at the barbecue.

As we stood chatting, I kept thinking about asking if anyone else was getting more food, but I just couldn't bring myself to say it. I stayed quiet and tried to carry on as normal. Eventually, I did manage to get a drink, and I was grateful for a warm cup of tea. It filled my stomach a little and gave me some comfort; it was better than nothing, especially since I hadn't eaten all day.

Luckily, they brought out pudding a bit later. There was rhubarb crumble with hot custard, and I jumped at the chance. I ate like there was no tomorrow. My friends just laughed as I wolfed it down, and I made a joke of it too, going back for seconds, pretending to show off, but really just giving myself a reason to eat more. I knew I wasn't going to get another proper meal until the next day. In the end, I felt good that night. Yes, I'd gone without dinner, but I'd still managed to turn up, join in, and feel like I belonged, even if only a little. A few months earlier, before I started working at the garage, I wouldn't have had the courage to arrive late or stay at all. It felt like progress, and for once, I allowed myself to feel a quiet sense of achievement.

Chapter 6: Learning to Speak

I had started working most days and even popped into work when I wasn't scheduled, just to chat. While there, I'd often help serve customers anyway. It was a Sunday, and I was working with Cole, which absolutely pleased me. We'd grown close, and I genuinely looked forward to our shifts together. We often slipped out back behind the supermarket for a cigarette, and I'd take a ride on his moped. We chatted about anything and everything; he could talk as much as I could. Despite being painfully shy, he always seemed at ease with me, and I reckon he must have picked up the same vibe about me when we first met. The conversation between us always flowed naturally, and from the beginning, we just felt comfortable around each other.

That Sunday, we only had a short four-hour shift, so we knew we'd have time for a quick fag out back and a spin on the bike. I had once told myself I was going to get a bike of my own, but deep down I suppose I didn't have the real passion to follow through with it.

I had always dreamed of having a car. It amazed me that you could just get into a vehicle and drive anywhere you wanted. At fifteen, I didn't fully understand the cost of owning one, but the idea of that freedom captivated me. There was a very beautiful girl, about five years older than me, around my sister's age, who would often come into the

61

garage for fuel. I used to watch her and think how pretty she was and how one day, I wanted to be like her: free to go anywhere I chose. I dreamed of leaving the area, not anywhere specific, just away.

That morning, I got ready for work feeling excited, though slightly annoyed with myself for not arranging to meet Cole earlier. We'd never met before work, but I didn't see the difference, considering we usually went out for a cigarette afterwards. Still, never mind. On my way in, I popped into the local shop and bought some chewing gum. When I arrived at work, I only had to wait around ten minutes for Daniel to show up and unlock the shop. The mechanics didn't work Sundays, so it was mostly just me and Cole on shift.

Cole arrived just after me. He looked a bit sheepish, and I asked him why. He simply said, "I'll tell you later." I said okay, not sure what he was up to. From the moment we opened, customers started coming in, and we were quickly swept up in the busyness of it all. I didn't have much time to talk to Cole properly. One of our regulars, the same man who'd waved at me from the car window when I got soaked, came in to buy cigarettes. I asked if he'd gotten any fuel, and he said no. He came in a couple of times a week, usually with a friend, always beeping the horn when they passed. Even though it had become more familiar, I still cringed slightly when I saw him.

As I was serving him, another customer came in needing parts, so I apologised to the man and said, "Sorry, I have to serve this guy. Do you want anything else?" He said no and walked out.

I moved to the other side of the shop, dreading what the new customer might ask for. I hated the parts section; it was never something I felt confident with. To be honest, I usually got Cole to handle it and bribed him with offers to make the tea. Cole liked tea just as much as I did, and I must've made a decent cuppa, because he always asked me to make it.

The kitchen was at the back, down a narrow corridor. There was a boiler on the wall and a cupboard full of cups, with tea, coffee, and milk kept in the fridge. Everything was a bit grubby, mugs stained with oil, surfaces marked with greasy handprints. The mechanics would come in with oily fingers, and although they wiped their hands quickly, the mess always remained. But honestly, it didn't bother me. The floor tiles were black, all scuffed and worn out, but I suppose that was just part of garage life. I actually liked making tea. I never had to worry about keeping the place too tidy, because no matter how much you cleaned, it never looked clean. Sometimes, when things were quiet and Cole was minding the shop, I'd have a go at cleaning it up anyway.

When I came back with the tea, Cole had a massive smirk plastered across his face.

"What?" I asked, narrowing my eyes.

He didn't answer right away, and I suddenly remembered he'd been trying to tell me something earlier in the day. Now I was curious.

"What was it you wanted to say this morning?" I pressed.

He grinned. "I can't remember now… but that guy? He's coming in to ask you out."

I just stood there, completely confused. "What are you on about?"

Then I saw him, the same guy from earlier. The one with the hand. He walked in through the door and, for the first time, I noticed how tall he was. Usually, he was just a passing blur, always sitting in his mate's car. I had served him earlier in the day, but I'd been distracted, too busy worrying about messing up with the bloke from the parts shop.

"You're lying," I said, glancing at Cole.

But he shook his head. "Why would a guy come in four times on a Sunday, not even for fuel, and once just for sweets?"

Oh my God. I was shocked. Actually, scared. The thought of being asked out made my stomach twist. Without thinking, I blurted, "I'll make the tea," and bolted out the back. This had happened once before and I'd completely messed it up. Now, the panic was all-consuming. I was so terrified that I started making the sign of the cross over my chest like some frantic plea to God to save me. And then, it happened. I looked up and there he was. The tall guy. The hand. Standing right there behind me.

Oh no. Had he seen me? Oh God, he had. He definitely had. What must he think? That I was some raving lunatic? What was I even thinking, why had I done that cross in the first place?

Mortified didn't even begin to cover it. There was no fixing this. None. So I did the only thing I could. I looked up, tried to keep my face neutral, and said, "Hi, you okay?" Like I hadn't just been doing a Mother Teresa impression when saving a dying sole.

Well, I wasn't sure if he'd heard me properly, but I think he was just as nervous as I was. Then he said, "Do you want to go out for a drink on Wednesday?" I said yes, and honestly, I wished he'd just hurry up and leave because I needed five minutes to gather my sanity after what had just happened. But he just stood there, and I couldn't understand why. I hadn't even thought about the fact he might need my address; I was too stressed to think straight. Then he asked, "What time do you finish work? Shall I pick you up from your house?"

I'd completely lost hold of my senses by that point, but I looked at him and said, "Yes, picking me up from my house is fine, I live—" and before I could finish, he cut in: "I know where you live. I went to school with your brother."

That completely knocked me off balance. He seemed to know me, yet I hadn't the faintest idea who he was or where he lived.

Trying to collect myself, I said, "I finish at eight, so I'll be ready for eight thirty, if that's okay."

"Yes," he replied, and just like that, he turned and walked off, as if he couldn't leave fast enough. It felt like he was gone in a flash. I stood there for a moment, wondering if I'd actually imagined the whole thing. Although, I wished I had imagined my Mother Teresa impression. I hadn't made the tea yet, so I called out to let Cole know I was still on it. When he didn't answer, I poked my head into the shop and saw he was out on the forecourt serving a customer. I quickly got on with the tea, I hadn't been too busy, but I liked to make sure I pulled my weight.

And then, just as I turned around, things took a more interesting turn. Cole was looking through the window at me, smirking, clearly eager for the gossip. He hurried in, grinning like mad.

"So, was I right?" he asked.

"Well... you might've been," I replied.

"Oh my God!" Cole gasped. "Tell me what happened!"

I shot him a look and said, "First off, you little shit bag, you let him through the back when I was being my usual weirdo self, drawing a cross on my chest. Then I looked up and saw him standing there!"

Cole burst out laughing. Proper tears-in-his-eyes laughing. He found it hysterical.

I, on the other hand, didn't find it quite so funny at first. But seeing Cole in stitches made me start to see the humour in it, and I actually began to laugh too.

"What did you say?" he asked. "That's so embarrassing! I'm surprised he still asked you out!"

I reached out to slap him playfully and shouted, "Thanks, mate!"

He gave me a reassuring smile and said, "So, when are you going out, mate?"

"He asked me to go out Wednesday," I said.

"Why Wednesday and not tonight?" Cole asked, raising an eyebrow.

I shrugged. "I don't know." Then I walked off to serve someone who was waiting for fuel—perfect timing, really.

The day passed quite quickly, as Sundays always did; we only worked four hours. Thinking back, when the guy asked me out, we must've already been halfway through the shift. Cole's earlier comment now made more sense. It did seem a bit obvious, in hindsight, he'd been in four times in two hours. And not once for fuel.

It was my turn to read the pump, and I suddenly felt embarrassed being outside, just in case the hand passed by. I felt more exposed, like he now knew I fancied him enough to agree to go for a drink. I took the readings, but one of them didn't match the till's takings, and Cole looked worried. I hadn't realised how shy and similar to me Cole was until that moment. Funnily enough, because he looked so scared, I felt brave enough to take the lead.

"It'll be fine, Cole. I'll sort it; maybe I read it wrong," I said, trying to reassure him. After all, I had been a bit stressed. I took the clipboard back outside and read the pump again. I had written it down wrong. This time, everything tallied up perfectly with the till. Cole made a joke, saying I was lovesick and that he'd be reading the pump from now on while I mopped the floors. He laughed.

"Okay, whatever," I replied, "at least I got it right now."

He grinned and said, "Wanna have a quick ciggy out back?"

I didn't really feel like it, but I rarely turned Cole down, so I said yes. "I've only got half an hour, though."

"Yeah, I'm in a rush too," he said, in that way men always do, like they've got something cooler going on.

I didn't actually have to be home, but I was excited about being asked out. I just wanted to get home, have a bit of time to think it all over, and enjoy the feeling on my own.

Cole wheeled his moped around the back of the supermarket, and I asked, "Can I have a go?"

He smiled. "Yeah, if you give me a cigarette."

I threw him a pack of twenty Benson & Hedges. "Wow, someone's flush," he said with a laugh.

I laughed too, started the engine, and I was off. I only went slow; the car park wasn't that big, but it felt fast enough to me. I was starting to feel quite confident. I did a few laps before stopping next to Cole.

"Pass me one of those, then," I said.

He threw me the pack, and I added, "And a light!"

He stood up, pulled a lighter from his pocket, and flicked the lid open; it was a Zippo, one of those posh lighters you can use in the wind without the flame going out.

I thought I should get myself one of those.

The flame was huge. "Careful, you nearly singed my hair!" I shouted. "Lucky, I haven't used my usual hairspray today; I'd have gone up like a bonfire!"

I got off the bike, parked it on its stand, and sat next to Cole while I finished my cigarette. We'd been out there about forty-five minutes, and although I hadn't meant to stay that long, I had enjoyed his company. Riding the bike was probably just the distraction I needed.

Eventually, I stood up. "Well, mate, I'll see you tomorrow night."

"I'll be there after college," he said. "Might be a bit late. Cover for me?"

I gave him a reassuring smile. "I got you," I said with a wink and a laugh, then walked off towards home. I never bothered getting a lift on Sundays anyway; we finished at two, and it was only a short walk.

I looked down the road and spotted the chip shop. The hand's friend's car was parked outside, and instantly my heart started to race. I felt naked, exposed, and I hated it. I suddenly felt so stupid and vulnerable, and it hit me just how unsettling that feeling could be. For a second, I genuinely considered turning around and walking nearly three miles out of my way just to avoid passing him. That would mean going back to work and taking the long route home, but at least I wouldn't have to face this. I had a quiet word with myself: What's the worst that can happen? I took a breath, crossed the road and told myself, just look at the car, see if they're looking, and wave, like a normal human being. I had about a hundred thoughts racing through my mind: Will he call? Will they notice me? What if they ignore me? What if I wave and look like an idiot? I looked up. The hand casually stretched his arm out of the window. Phew. That was easier than I'd imagined. I waved and walked on as casually as I could manage, even though nothing about how I felt inside was casual. I felt like a wobbly piece of jelly, and I was probably walking all crooked and looking ridiculous. But I'd made it past and I was still alive.

Flipping heck, what a strange day it had been. I'd only been out of the house for four hours, but it felt like my whole life was changing in front of me. This morning, I'd left home just looking forward to working with Cole. Now I had a date with the hand. Someone actually fancied me enough to ask me out. I didn't want to think too much about it, or I'd get overwhelmed and start to panic. And there it was, the sudden realisation: I was going to have to think about what to wear. I didn't have many clothes. I'd worked most of my life and never really had a social one. I made my way home quicker after seeing the hand, and then it hit me: I didn't even know the guy's name. Oh. My. God. How embarrassing. How was I going to get around that? Then again, I hadn't told him my name either. But he seemed to know who I was, so maybe he already knew it. Well, I wasn't going to let a small detail like not knowing his name ruin this for me. I'd probably just lose a couple of hours' sleep over it. If I was lucky, I might still get six.

As I went through the front door, my dad was just heading into the toilet and mentioned I was late home. Now what? Should I tell him about my date on Wednesday? Hell yes. As soon as he came out of the toilet, I blurted out, "I got asked out today, and I'm going out after work on Wednesday."

"Oh yeah?" he said. "Who's the boy? What's his name?"

Oh crap, how could I tell my dad I didn't actually know his name? I quickly changed the subject, pretending I hadn't said anything.

"What's for dinner, Dad? Do you know?"

"Your mum's plated it up; it's in the oven. Chicken today."

"Oh great," I said, rushing past him, hoping he'd forget all about the mention of the date.

But of course, he didn't. "Well, about this boy—" he began.

"He's a friend of my brother's," I interrupted quickly.

"Oh, great," Dad said, and that was the end of the conversation. The fact that he was my brother's friend seemed to kibosh Dad's interest.

My first love had been my brother's best mate, although I actually think they hadn't been all that close until he started coming around for me. Their friendship seemed to grow alongside our relationship. It only lasted about six months, but I was completely heartbroken when it ended. Even now, I still held a bit of a candle for him. Any mention of his name made me feel a bit wobbly. I'd always try to be nearby if I knew he was around, unless he had a girlfriend in tow, which he did a couple of times, much to my disgust.

Still, I had a date now, and it felt lovely being in my own little world again. Funny thing was, I hadn't really paid much attention to this new guy until recently. I'd only started waving to him around May or June, even though I'd been working there since January. He must've passed by quite a few times; that would explain why he asked me out.

I went into the kitchen to eat my dinner. It looked amazing. I shouted, "Thanks, Mum!"

Dad shouted back, "She's out!"

"Oh," I said, not thinking much of it, and grabbed my knife and fork.

"Aren't you going to heat it up?" Dad called from the other room.

"Nah, I like it lukewarm," I replied, already munching. Mum had been generous with the chicken, five roast potatoes, and loads of veg. She'd started making me proper dinners since I began working so much. Maybe she missed me. Or maybe she thought I needed the food. Truthfully, I was eating loads of chocolate these days and had put on quite a bit of weight.

When I worked with Cole, I used to wear shorts and wobble my thighs, saying, "Look at that wobble." He'd blush and say, "You're crazy."

He wasn't far wrong. I didn't have a great body image, and I hadn't for a long time. It started during the abuse; I stopped liking how I felt in my own body. Gaining weight reminded me of the times he touched me, especially anything tight around my thighs or crotch. I liked myself as a person, but I felt uncomfortable in my skin; that's the best way I can explain it. I was growing taller, though, and sometimes the weight would go on and come off again without me needing to diet. I was five foot six now, but only a year ago I'd been taken out of class to be measured. That last year at school, I grew nearly a foot, and that was when the abuse had finally stopped. I've always wondered if that's why I didn't grow until then.

I stayed in with Dad for the rest of the day, as Mum was out until late. We watched a western. Well, Dad was actually watching it while I was just relishing his company. I sat there feeling genuinely happy and content. To my surprise, I found I quite liked westerns, although I doubt I would've ever sat through one on my own. In the film, they were herding cattle and riding horses, and the cowboys weren't bad to look at either, I suppose. Clint Eastwood featured in quite a few of the films Dad liked. In truth, I didn't really care much for the television. What I did care about was spending time with Dad. Being one of four children, it was rare to have either parent to yourself. The only time you really got to be alone with Mum was if you offered to go food shopping with her. But even then, she was too busy with the shopping to notice if you were there or not, though I would sometimes sneak a treat into the trolley and hope she wouldn't notice until the checkout. But now, I earned my own money. I didn't need Mum to buy me little treats anymore. Speaking of earnings, I used to throw my wages into the top drawer of my chest, and it was already half full. The truth was, I didn't need much. Mum still bought my clothes, though not many, since I was either at school or work most days, where I wore the same jeans and jumper my sister had bought me. My middle sister had started buying me clothes too, once she got a job. She'd realised Mum never bought us anything fashionable and felt sorry for me. Even my eldest sister chipped in, buying me clothes for Christmas now that she was working as well.

I went into my bedroom to see what I actually had to wear on Wednesday. I wasn't too bothered about jeans; worn jeans were in fashion anyway, but I was worried about tops. I didn't have many, and I didn't really wear them. I preferred to live in my oversized jumper. It swamped my body, hid my bum, and made me look thinner than I was. I pulled open the top drawer. There was a plain white top; nah, not wearing that. Underneath it was an orange top I'd completely forgotten about. It had a crew neck. I thought about it for a moment and then decided against that too. I rummaged through just about everything in the drawer and still felt like I had nothing to wear. That settled it, I'd ask Mum to wash my jumper. At least then it would be clean.

Everyone wore jumpers anyway. It was July, yes, but it was England, and it could definitely be jumper weather, especially in the evening. We weren't going out until eight-thirty.

By the time I'd finished wrestling with my clothes and thrown everything back into the drawers, it was getting quite late. I went into the lounge, said goodnight to Dad, and noticed Mum still wasn't home. I made myself a cup of tea and one for Dad, too. My parents never said no to a cuppa. I took my cup back to my room, clearing my bed by chucking everything onto the floor, usually the nicely folded, ironed clothes Mum had left out for me to put away. I never knew why she bothered. I always threw them on the floor and left them there until I wore them or threw them back in the wash without ever putting them on.

As I climbed into bed—shit—I spilled my tea all over the duvet. Flip, shit, I muttered as I turned the duvet around so the wet part was at the foot end. Still better than lying in a puddle of tea. I told myself I'd take the cover off in the morning, knowing full well I wouldn't. Mum would see it and end up changing it. I struggled enough just getting up in the morning; changing a duvet? Not happening. I didn't even make myself breakfast or lunch most days, so the chances of me sorting out a duvet were slim. Now I fancied another cup of tea; I'd barely had a sip. I went back into the kitchen. Dad called out, asking if it was me. Maybe he thought Mum had come in without him hearing the door.

"No, it's just me; I spilt my tea," I shouted back. "I'm just making another one. Do you want one?"

"Of course," he said. I made two and trotted back off to bed quickly before Dad's mood changed; he could turn quite quickly, especially when he was waiting for Mum to get home.

At least I could have a lie-in now, with school finished. I only worked part-time at the garage. Although, I had offered to do a full day on Monday, something I'd completely forgotten about until I opened my eyes and looked at the time. Damn. I had to be there by nine, and it was already eight-forty. There was no time for a shower. I grabbed some clothes off the floor, not my favourite jumper, though; that was in the laundry now. I settled for a T-shirt instead. Miraculously, the sun was out; it actually felt hot for the first time this year. I even considered wearing shorts, but there was no time now. I'd have to run even if I left that second.

As I left the house, I wondered who I'd be working with. Not Cole; he was only part-time and still in college. It'd be Liz, my sister's friend, I thought, as I turned the corner and saw into the shop. She looked up and gave me a huge grin. She was always smiling—that was just Liz— and it was a nice welcome. I was glad to see her. I enjoyed working with her. She'd always ask about my life, my future, and what I wanted to do. She'd once mentioned the idea of working at the garage full-time but also said I should try something else, that she thought I could do better. That made me feel warm inside. I didn't believe it for a second; my mum had always called me thick and said I was like her.

But still, it was nice. Nice that someone thought I could do better.

It was a quiet day, and Liz had spent the longest time upstairs with management. Not that I minded; I quite liked serving the customers. Well, mostly. Unless they were lecherous, like some were. You could see them staring at your arse as you bent over to fill the tank. Whenever I noticed, I'd pull a face and turn around with a look that said, pervert. Most of the men who did it were far too old to be looking at me like that. Given my past, I used to feel physically sick at the thought. But in reality, I'd just turn my back and push it out of my mind. I don't have to live with that pervert, I'd tell myself, and somehow that made it easier to ignore. To be fair, it wasn't that common, which helped. I even knew the regular offender by now, so when I worked with Cole, I'd usually send him out to deal with him. He probably saw me working and used that as an excuse to fill up. Actually, no, that's a lie. He only ever put in a fiver at a time. Tight bastard, I thought. He didn't look like he could afford much more. He drove an old banger that was falling to pieces. Put it this way: I'm no snob, but I wouldn't have been seen dead in that car.

I'd just finished serving someone when Ryan pulled up. Shit, I thought. He was my first love, and I immediately felt nervous. Now I wished Liz were here to serve him instead. Even though I often saw him and we still spoke now and then, I didn't want to be the one putting fuel in his car. It felt horrible, awkward, even. I slipped into the shop, hoping to avoid it altogether. But I knew he'd probably seen me on the forecourt and was wondering where I'd disappeared to. Since it was a service garage, customers came into the shop to ask for fuel. When I saw that Liz still hadn't come down, I knew it was only a matter of time before he walked through the door. I'd have no choice but to serve him. I tried to make myself look busy, shifting the sweets around like I hadn't noticed him. Then I heard the door chime; it was loud on purpose to alert us when someone came in. We didn't want anyone in the shop unsupervised, especially not school kids passing through on their way home. To be honest, I never understood why they bought sweets at the garage. They were much more expensive than at the supermarket. But that's kids for you; they didn't have to earn their money, so it was easy come, easy go. Especially when it came to crisps, chocolate bars, and sweets. The garage was right next to the school, so it was convenient. They were probably starving after the school day, not for proper food, just sugar. And we sold everything they craved. My boss used to claim he didn't make any money on the fuel, but he certainly made up for it by emptying the pockets of the parents.

I looked up on autopilot, even though I already knew who it was. With my back still turned, I said, "I'll be right there." But to my surprise, he kept walking towards me. I turned to face him and said coolly, "Hey."

He replied, "I hear you've got a date with Dan."

I felt a flicker of annoyance that he'd even brought it up. "Yes, I do actually," I said. "And I'm really looking forward to it."

He asked, "Have you seen my brother?"

"No, why?" I replied. Then I added, "Although he should be finishing work soon. He usually pops into the shops and stuffs himself with doughnuts on the way home. I pass him all the time when I'm heading to work. Has he ever once given me a doughnut? No."

But that was just typical of my brother. There wasn't much 'brotherly love' in our family, even though I only had the one. The only Christmas present he ever gave me was a teddy he'd originally bought for his girlfriend before she dumped him just before Christmas.

"There you go," I thought. "You can leave now, Ryan."

"Thanks," he said, heading out of the shop.

I wondered if the mention of my date had made him feel even a little jealous. I really hoped it had. At least now I knew the name of 'the hand', without needing to ask. Strange though, that he shared the same name as my boss. Still, I supposed it made things easier; I was already used to the name.

Despite all that, I'd found myself thinking about Ryan less and less lately, especially with my date coming up. Then Cole pulled up outside on his moped, and Liz made a point of putting on a bit of a show.

"Right then," she said with a big Cheshire cat grin. "I'll leave you two to it. Don't work too hard." She gave me a cheeky wink and walked out the door. I didn't mind. Out of everyone, I preferred working with Cole the most.

"Hi," I greeted him. "I'll get this one; you make the tea."

He agreed and went into the kitchen to take off his helmet and leather jacket. Typical boys, always so protective of their helmets and jackets. But I supposed they weren't cheap, and they were necessary for saving lives.

I ran outside to serve a car. "How much fuel would you like?" I asked.

"Ten pounds, please."

I repeated it back: "Ten pounds?"

"Yes, please," they confirmed.

But when they went in to pay, they walked up to Cole at the till and said, "Fiver, please."

I stepped in, "Sorry, you asked for ten."

He refused to pay and said, "Go get your boss."

Cole looked nervous, but I wasn't rattled. I knew I'd done everything properly, even repeating it back. So, I went to get Daniel, the boss, and Cole was left with the man.

I explained what happened, and Daniel said, "They try it on sometimes. I'll sort it. You did repeat the amount, right?"

I nodded, following him back like I was in trouble. But when we got there, the customer had already left. Cole said, "He just chucked the tenner at me and walked off saying we didn't know what we were doing."

Daniel gave a satisfied nod. "That's because he knew you were right. Well done, Mandy; good work looking after my money."

I felt proud. Though it did make me think, what actual proof did I ever really have? Even if I repeated it back, it was still my word against theirs. But I guessed as an employee, the boss would back me, and the customer wouldn't risk being barred from the garage. So in the end, they usually just paid up.

Anyway, the rest of the shift flew by, and soon I was walking home. I felt shattered. I'd basically worked the whole day alone, and I was really looking forward to a quiet evening. When I got home, I had some of Mum's lovely homemade chicken pie, then headed straight to bed. I had Tuesday off, and I planned to lie in and do absolutely nothing. I could sleep like a log and probably wouldn't wake until midday. Once I was in bed, I did what I always did; I began imagining rescue stories to help me drift off. It was my little routine.

When I woke up, the house was completely silent. Everyone was out at work. I didn't mind the peace. I got up and headed to the kitchen to make a cuppa tea—obviously. I just hoped Dad wasn't in bed on a night shift. If I woke him, he'd get really cross. He never hit me, except once with a belt when I was naughty, but back then, that was considered normal. It was the shouting that scared me more. It always left me feeling small and shaken. I don't know why exactly, but it made me feel like he didn't like me. And what I really wanted, more than anything, was love and cuddles. I longed for something to fill the deep insecurities left behind by all the abuse.

The garden looked quite dull for a July day, but that was normal. The sun usually came around a bit later in the day. It was mostly south-facing, and there was a tree in the middle of the garden with the sunbathing chairs right under it for shade. Mum often sunbathed in the garden; it was very secluded, which was just as well because she usually had her breast out. I found it completely normal, having grown up with this behaviour, though I doubted my friends would have felt the same. They never mentioned it, though.

I walked back into the bedroom, got back into bed, and chilled out for a while. It wasn't until I caught sight of the sun outside my window that I realised it was already two o'clock. I knew the sun didn't come round until midday, so I opened the curtains to check, and sure enough, Dad's car wasn't there. Great, I thought. If he had been home, he would've got cross with me for still being in bed. I got dressed and made myself some toast. At least I only had three hours to waste before work. That evening, while walking home from work, I found myself imagining the date and feeling really good about it. As I neared the end of my close, I looked up and saw a cyclist. I recognised the hand, Dan, and my heart started beating so fast it felt like there was no tomorrow. I timed it in my head and knew he'd reach me before I reached the turning into my road and would disappear from sight. I was about to look away, pretending I hadn't noticed him, when he waved me to stop. I felt much calmer than I had imagined and certainly calmer than when I'd drawn the cross over my chest earlier. I stopped as he'd signalled, waiting for him to catch up. He looked even better than I'd first thought. I asked him where he'd been, and he said he'd been at the launderette, doing his washing. Oddly, he didn't have any washing with him, but I didn't mention it. I just said, "Oh, that sounds boring."

It made me wonder—did he live alone? When I asked, he confirmed he did, and that felt a little scary. Here I was, going out with someone who didn't live with their parents.

We had been chatting for about an hour, and I kept thinking about inviting him back, but I didn't quite have the confidence. I wasn't secure enough about the connection to risk rejection at that point. Still, the thought kept overwhelming me and, embarrassingly, was making me look like I wasn't really listening.

Before I knew it, he asked, "What are you up to now?"

"I've just finished work," I replied. And without thinking, the words just slipped out: "You can walk back to mine if you like and have a cuppa."

Oh my God, I thought. Did I just say that? I could feel the tension in my throat.

He smiled and said, "Okay, I'll stay for one. It'll be fine."

I felt really happy. It was strange; I hadn't really noticed this guy for months, and suddenly, I fancied him like mad.

As we started walking towards my house, I began to worry. What if my parents said something? But then I reminded myself I was sixteen now. Surely, they wouldn't mind.

Chapter 7: Invisible Wounds

When we arrived, I took a deep breath and led him inside. Luckily, my parents were out. My brother was in his bedroom, and he gave a casual "hello" when he saw us; he and this guy had gone to school together. They hadn't been friends, not really, but they knew of each other. We went into the lounge, and I asked him what he'd like to drink. "A cup of tea," he said, "two sugars, white." I nodded and went into the kitchen, quietly relieved to have a moment to myself. Being alone with him had made me nervous. I hadn't had many relationships before, and it had been a while since I'd gone out with Ryan. That had felt different; we'd spent time around each other at the local café with my sister, and my siblings knew him. It felt safer, more familiar. But this was different. I didn't know this guy at all, although I did feel a bit more at ease knowing that my brother at least knew of him.

As I made the tea, I began doubting myself again. Was I reading this all wrong? The pressure I put on myself felt immense. When I walked back in and handed him the cup, I felt surprisingly more relaxed. We started chatting again, and I sat down next to him; our thighs touched. The conversation flowed so easily. We laughed, joked, and he was just… easy to talk to. He started teasing me a little, gently tickling me, and I found myself enjoying it. Then, his hand found mine and instead of pulling away, he left it there. It felt intense, but good. He turned to look at me. His eyes met mine, and before I knew it, he was leaning in. Our lips touched, and I soon felt his tongue inside my mouth. I felt hot and excited, and I moved my tongue around his, trying to connect with him in some deeper way. My mind went silent. All I could focus on was the sensation, the warmth of his breath, the feel of his lips and tongue. I suddenly needed to come up for air. Our embrace broke, and I was too shy to meet his eyes. Instead, I nestled into his side for a hug, placing my head on his shoulder, an escape from having to face the man who had just taken my breath away.

He stayed still, like he understood. He gave me a moment to compose myself, and it felt more comforting than I'd imagined. Soon, we were chatting and laughing again, as if nothing had happened. It felt natural. I didn't want the evening to end. I was scared he might say he had to go. It was late, and he probably had work the next day. Then, he smiled and told me something that surprised me. He admitted that he had purposefully timed his walk past my road that evening, hoping he'd bump into me. I laughed and asked, "Then why did you ask me out for Wednesday if you wanted to see me earlier?"

He chuckled. "I don't get paid till Wednesday."

And just like that, it made perfect sense. Back then, it wasn't even a question; if a man asked you out, it was assumed he'd pay. That's just the way it was. Men were the breadwinners. They went to work while women often stayed home and looked after the children. And if a man asked you out, he was assumed to be your boyfriend until one of you ended it.

I could tell he was nearly ready to leave because his demeanour shifted, and he admitted he needed to get up early. He then told me he was going to see his mum the week after, which, surprisingly, made my heart sink a little. Even though I hadn't known him long, I was already missing him.

When he finally said he had to go, I walked him to the door. We stood there, cuddling, and then kissed. He pulled back and said, "I go out with my friends on Tuesdays." I said, "Okay." Then he added, "I'll see you Wednesday after work. I'm looking forward to it." Hearing this sent shivers down my spine. An excitement bubbled up inside me, and it felt strange; my life suddenly felt so much better than it had in a long time. I waved him off as he got back on his bike, then walked into my bedroom, which was right by the front door of the bungalow we lived in. In a way, I was glad he had gone. I needed a moment to gather my thoughts; it had all been so unexpected, and it had left me feeling drained. When I looked at my bed, I saw Mum had changed my sheets and placed my clothes on top, my jumper and jeans for tomorrow's date. The fact that I already knew what I was wearing made me feel a little better, and it felt comforting now. I was relieved we'd spent this time together. He'd let me know tonight that the date was actually a foursome, and I would be meeting his friend's girlfriend. That scared me somewhat, but after everything we'd shared tonight, I felt more prepared to face it.

I felt grown up. As I lay down and rested my head on the pillow, I didn't need to make up one of my usual stories that night; I had a real one to live, for a change. The thought was comforting, and before I knew it, I had drifted off and was waking up around midday the next day. I went for a walk that afternoon, just wandering around aimlessly. I realised I didn't much like not having school. Even though I used to complain about it constantly, I now saw how it kept me busy. Without it, the days felt slower, and I found myself wishing time would pass more quickly. I didn't work on Tuesdays, and Laura was still in school since she was a year younger than me.

Before I knew it, Wednesday had arrived. I got ready for work, feeling both anxious and excited. The idea of chatting to Cole about my evening with Dan helped settle my nerves. I had somehow managed not to overthink the date until now, although I had already laid out the clothes I would wear, my favourite baggy jumper and jeans that Mum had just washed. I'd had to make do with my other pair lately, the ones that were uncomfortably tight around the crotch. They used to stretch with wear, but I suspected I had put on a bit of weight, and now they didn't budge. It made me feel self-conscious and a bit low. But today was different; I had my good jeans back; the ones I wore practically twenty-four-seven when I wasn't working. Probably like most other sixteen-year-olds. Oh yes, I had turned sixteen back in May. Not quite "Sweet Sixteen and never been kissed"; we won't get into that. And yes, it was Ryan, if you're wondering.

When I arrived at work, I looked around for Cole. I was genuinely excited to tell him everything, but I couldn't see him. Then Daniel, the boss, said, "He's not in tonight;

he's stuck at college. I'll be upstairs. Just give me a shout if you need anything." My heart sank with disappointment.

Still, as it turned out, the shop got busy not long after I arrived. I was filling car after car, one right after the other. It was steady but manageable, and I didn't need to call for help. Before I knew it, it was time to go home. In a way, I was glad I hadn't seen Cole; I'd have even more to tell him on Friday when he was next in. At least, I thought he would be. He didn't even know about Monday night yet. He'd love that bit; he was such a gossip. Whether the stories he told were true or not didn't seem to matter; I always found them entertaining. We talked all the time, yet knew very little about each other personally. I suppose that was the appeal: an escape from our home lives. It suited me fine.

At the end of my shift, I took the clipboard and began writing down the pump numbers. Daniel called out, "Do you want a lift home?" I shouted back, "No, thanks."

Even though I'd spent Monday night with Dan the hand, I still felt nervous all over again. I was going to be meeting more of his friends tonight, and I couldn't help but worry about whether they'd like me, especially not Mark, because I already knew him and he seemed nice, but his girlfriend. Her name was Lynn, and she was older than me. In those days, even a couple of years' age difference felt significant. Once I got home, I rushed into the shower, only to be greeted by freezing cold water. Every hair on my body stood on end, and I shivered all over, but I stayed in and washed my hair anyway. I must really like this guy, I thought. I'm willingly enduring a freezing cold shower just to be ready in time. There was no time to wait for the water to warm up. I grabbed two towels from the cupboard, dropped another one by accident, and didn't bother picking it up. I ran, half-naked, down the corridor to my room. There was no time to be modest; I had to get ready. I quickly did my hair, skipped makeup as usual, and with only five minutes to spare, I saw the car pull up outside. I felt breathless. Dan and Mark were in the front, which meant I'd be in the back all alone with the girlfriend, Lynn.

Dan had just gotten out of the car and started walking up the drive when I saw Lynn getting out and switching places with him. A wave of relief washed over me. As I got into the car, everyone greeted me with a cheerful "hello," and I noticed that Lynn looked really friendly, which made me feel better. Dan, usually shy, was full of energy tonight. He announced, "We're going to the Friendly Pork Pie," and everyone burst into laughter. I didn't quite get the joke, but it didn't matter. The pub, it turned out, was called "The Happy Cheese", and they were all laughing because I didn't know the name of the pub. I suppose I hadn't spent much time in pubs, being only sixteen. My life had mostly revolved around work and school until recently, and now just part-time work. I didn't drive, so pubs hadn't really been accessible to me before.

I smiled, and, to my surprise, I felt comfortable being laughed at. When I realised the joke, I joined in with their laughter. It made sense now, and I felt more included. I looked at Dan, and he took my hand, holding it as though to protect me and reassure me. It was as if he were saying, "You're safe with me." And in that moment, I felt exactly that—safe. Despite everything being so far beyond my usual experiences, it felt manageable, even comforting. I edged closer to him, and he drew me in for a kiss. The two people in the front groaned at us kissing, which only made me feel more at ease. I suddenly felt like I belonged, and it was a really good feeling. I looked at Dan; his hair looked nice, all fluffy with a wave to it, and he was wearing a pink jumper. I decided to turn the tables and tease him a little. "Did you not get your washing done, then? Looks like you're wearing your sister's jumper."

At that, everyone burst into laughter again. Dan laughed too, squeezing my hand as if to say he was proud of me for making the effort to fit in. It felt right, being there, all of us laughing together.

We reached the pub, and Dan asked what I'd like to drink. I said, "An orange juice, please." He replied, "You can have alcohol," but I couldn't bear the thought of being questioned, asked to leave, and having everyone else leave because of me. I just said, "No, orange juice is good, thanks."

Although it was probably the cheaper option, men usually paid for drinks, and I always felt uncomfortable about that. I never took advantage. I generally kept to the same drink all night. Not that I minded; I enjoyed simply being out and doing something different. I'd never needed a lot in life, and I rarely spent my wages. Money wasn't something I had grown used to using. I didn't care much for it and never worked to earn it for its own sake. It was just a bonus from working, and I'd toss it into a drawer. After I left school, my parents started charging me to live at home. I paid eight pounds a week, which seemed steep, especially since my siblings only paid ten, despite earning over a hundred. My dad assured me it cost the same regardless of earnings. I didn't mind, though. I liked paying my way; it made me feel more grown up.

As we sat there, I suddenly realised I needed the toilet but felt too shy to ask where it was. I hadn't been to enough pubs to feel confident walking around on my own, especially since I didn't know Dan that well yet. Dan noticed something was off and asked if I was alright. I whispered, "I need the toilet," and, funnily enough, he understood straight away. He offered to come with me since he needed to go too. I was grateful for the offer.

As he stood up, he said, "We're off to the loo, and I'll get another round in. What do you both want?" Lynn asked for a snowball, and Mark, who was driving, asked for a bitter shandy. Dan ordered one too. I declined, saying I still had the other one, but he said, "I'll buy you another," and just did it without asking again. Little signs were starting to build in my mind: he was kind. Even though he was loud, funny, and often teased, he had a sensitivity about him. He always made me feel like I was safe in his company. That sense of protection made me relax, even cheeky at times, and we often teased each other.

Soon it was time to go home, and I was secretly hoping he wouldn't just drop me off. As much as I liked his friends, I longed to be alone with him again, to cuddle and feel the closeness of his touch. To kiss, to feel his arms around me. I hadn't even thought about sex at this point; I just wanted to feel wanted and held.

It Is Not How Life Starts, It Is How You

Finish It

Chapter 8: The Long Road to Healing

As we got closer to home, I felt a quiet relief when Dan said to Mark, "Just drop me at Mandy's, and I'll make my own way back from there." Mark laughed and said, "Alright, lovebirds, don't give Lynn any ideas." I grabbed Dan's hand in response, a small signal that I appreciated what he'd said. His keenness to be alone with me comforted me. But as we pulled up, I saw my parents' car in the driveway, and my heart dropped. I wondered if Dad would still be awake and hoped he wasn't. Unfortunately, as we walked in, he was standing in the hallway. He reached out his hand and said, "You must be Dan." Dan shook it and said, "Yes, that's me."

"Well, I'll wish you both goodnight; I'm off to bed," Dad added, and I couldn't believe my luck. I loved my dad to bits, but I wasn't quite ready for him to meet my boyfriend, not at this early stage.

He'd embarrassed me enough back when I was going out with Ryan, and I didn't want a repeat of that. The day I met Ryan, I had been feeling really low and lonely. My elder sister, who had gone through similar feelings, looked after me. I'd been sitting on a bench just down the road from our house when she called Ryan and told him I was feeling suicidal. We'd seen him at the café we visited regularly, and he'd started offering us lifts. That day, he parked near the bench, unbeknown to me what my sister had told him, and started chatting. I felt both excited and

94

scared. It was awkward, and I had no experience in situations like that.

He chatted for a while, and when he offered me a ride in his car, it felt comforting and safe. We talked for ages, and then he asked if I wanted to go to the pub. The question startled me, not because I didn't want to go, but because I knew my dad probably wouldn't let me. I desperately wanted to go, but I hesitated. I stayed silent for a moment, unsure of how to respond.

As if on cue, my sister appeared. "I want to go, but Dad won't let me," I told her, feeling a sense of relief in her presence. With her there, I felt bolder, like I could act more like myself. Before she arrived, I had been too scared to answer, not wanting to say no, but also knowing deep down that I would probably be forbidden.

My sister reassured me, "I'll go, of course. I'll tell Dad, and you'll be fine." We sat in the car, waiting for confirmation from her. Then, out of nowhere, I saw my dad walking towards the car. My stomach dropped. This was the best I had felt in years, the least lonely, the most alive, and it felt like it was about to be taken from me before it had even begun. Dad popped his head into the car and asked, "What's this I hear? You want to go out tonight?" I looked down, feeling small, and quietly answered, "Yes, please." He paused, then said, "Go on then, if you don't want to be with me anymore."

I squirmed in my seat, pretending I hadn't heard him right. His words stung more than I'd expected.

"Thanks," I managed to say, and then he shouted at Ryan, "Get her home before ten o'clock!"

Though it was earlier than the time I had originally hoped for, I was still in shock that he had actually said yes. I looked at Ryan, silently pleading with him to just drive and get me away from this uncomfortable moment. As we drove down the road, I found myself wondering what Dad would say when I got home. But, to be honest, I no longer let these things bother me.

So here I was with Dan, and it felt good. We chatted all night, and he told me he was going away the following week and wouldn't be able to see me until he got back. A wave of sadness washed over me, but I was still happy that he wanted to continue seeing me; that in itself felt reassuring. We held hands and cuddled, which was incredibly comforting, and I realised I hadn't felt this happy in a very long time. When it was time for him to go home, we stood on the porch, and I found myself quietly anticipating our kiss. He leaned in, and before I knew it, our lips were touching. I opened my mouth, still slightly shy despite not being entirely new to kissing him. It had just been a while since I had felt this way or found myself in such a moment. Then I felt his tongue, and surprisingly, it seemed to fit in my mouth as though it belonged there. I couldn't taste anything distinct; it was as if it were part of my own saliva. We playfully explored the moment, and then he pulled back and began to tickle me. It was light-hearted and spontaneous. I felt whole, like everything was right in that moment.

But the truth is, I should have felt complete on my own, secure in myself and my worth, without needing someone else to feel whole. Sadly, that wasn't the case. Once he left, the loneliness crept in again. These were the days of house phones, so there was no easy contact between meetings. I counted the days he was away as if it were a lifetime. Insecurity started to grow. I worried he might change his mind and decide he didn't want to see me anymore. I tried to keep busy with work to distract myself. Meanwhile, conversations at home began turning to the subject of finding a full-time job. My mother called me 'thick', which hurt deeply. She had always viewed herself that way, and perhaps calling me the same made her feel less alone in her own belief. I'd done reasonably well at the garage job, I'd worked hard and felt comfortable there, but it hadn't shifted my self-esteem. That inner void remained untouched. I doubted everything, who I was, what I was worth. I looked at others and felt they had it all figured out. Not with jealousy, strangely, I never really felt that, but with a sense of quiet longing. I was happy for them, genuinely, but I wished I could feel as secure and content as they appeared to be.

The week dragged on, and while I enjoyed the moments at work, Dan had been gone six days, and I was starting to forget what he looked like. I missed him terribly and couldn't even remember exactly when I'd see him next. The time apart made me think about the future and the looming question of sex. I wondered how long it would be before he expected it. He had his own flat, and this scared me more because Ryan and I had had sex in our house, and my siblings were there. Well, obviously not in the same room, of course, but in the house, and I never felt scared.

To be honest, he had been a real gentleman and had waited approximately four months before having sex, and even then, he worried it might change things and asked if I was sure I wanted it. I at that time had felt I did want something different than the other experience I had had up until I was fifteen. I was scared, but not like when I was a child and growing up because it felt nicer actually wanting the boy to touch you and enjoying the touches. I had always felt a bit foolish because I was much younger than his last girlfriends, and he actually thought I was a year older than I was when he asked me out. When he found out I was fifteen and not sixteen as he had assumed. He said it wasn't right, and I understood. But his words still broke my heart. I cried, not just because I feared losing him, but because he had been such a comforting presence during a time when I felt deeply alone. That kind of care, being wanted and touched by someone you liked, was entirely different from the experiences I had endured growing up. For once, it had felt safe. It had felt wanted.

Since going out with him I felt liberated and although my grandad was still having sex with me, I felt stronger and more able to cope. I felt more wanted and cared for than I had before. Life had started to feel like it was finally moving forward for me. I no longer felt lonely and had developed a stronger relationship with my brother, thanks to his friendship with Ryan. I was even invited to join them for a night of fishing. However, this turned into a bit of a story in itself, as what should have been a beautiful evening was overshadowed by my worries about getting into trouble. We had spent the day out, and the boys had planned an overnight fishing trip, inviting me along. Even my brother seemed fine with the idea. I wrote a letter as my brother reassured me it would be okay. He told me, "Mandy, you're with me; they'll be fine." He also asked me to write a letter for them to read when they returned from visiting my father's brother. I really wanted to go, but I was nervous about not asking my parents face-to-face, which made me feel uncertain about the whole situation.

The letter said:

Mum and Dad I have gone all night fishing with Tim and Ryan and I will be back in the morning, I hope you don't mind but I couldn't ask you as you are at Aunty Alisons and Uncle Rob's.

It was quite a short letter, and while the boys were off fishing, I had time to worry about my parents discovering it. I began imagining my dad showing up, shouting at me in front of everyone. There was a group of us there, and the thought of being humiliated like that made my stomach turn. My imagination always had a way of running wild, especially when I knew things could go wrong—it was almost like I was always anticipating disaster. Not far from where we were, there was another girl down the beach, but she wasn't there for fishing, it was obvious they had gone there to have sex. Meanwhile, I sat quietly under a rock that jutted out from the sand. Ryan had laid out blankets for me to lie on, and I sat there, having these terrifying thoughts. Still, he kept checking on me, coming back every now and then to make sure I was okay. And I was, because it felt nice to be invited out by the boys, to feel included. It felt especially good to be out with my brother too. It was as if I had begun to build a life of my own, and that was quite an amazing feeling. Eventually, the boys started messing around and joking with each other. Ryan came over and cuddled up next to me, mostly to get warm, but we were laughing and enjoying ourselves. Then my brother started calling out for him, which annoyed me a little because I was having a nice moment with Ryan. He went to see what his friend wanted and came back saying we should pack up; Mack and his girlfriend were heading to the car park and we'd all meet there for a beer. I agreed, although I was still worried. The thought of my dad turning up and embarrassing me in front of everyone stuck in my mind. I feared it might put Ryan off me, especially if he thought my life was too dramatic or childish.

When we reached the car park, everyone got out except me. I stayed in the car. The other girl was two years older; she already had a job, and I suddenly felt small and foolish. Like a silly little schoolgirl who didn't belong. Ryan had come to terms with the fact that I was younger than he first thought, but he dealt with it by joking around. He'd tease me in a playful way, and although I knew he didn't mean it cruelly, I also knew it was how he coped with the age gap. Still, it was better than the alternative, better than him breaking up with me. When he'd found out I was only fifteen, not sixteen like he'd assumed, it had clearly shaken him. But even though we had only been seeing each other for a couple of weeks, he hadn't ended things. I suppose he didn't love me, but he cared enough to want to keep seeing me, and that meant something. I imagine it still bothered him, especially with his friends having girlfriends who were older and working. I knew they probably teased him about me being so young and still at school. But for whatever reason, he stayed.

I never minded when he teased me, because when we were alone at home, he treated me so well. We would have deep conversations about how we felt, and it felt special to confide in each other. I shared with him that I had a blood transfusion through the womb, and he opened up about an issue with his hand. It was moments like these that made our relationship feel so meaningful. Despite the good moments we shared, the age gap and the challenges we faced eventually took their toll. My dad, especially, played a part in ending things. He would occasionally become angry and tell Ryan to treat me better, which understandably created tension.

As I waited for Dan to come back, I worked through the week. On Wednesday, while I was at work, Dan popped his head in to say he was busy and out with his friends on Thursday but would see me on Friday. Although my heart sank at the thought of waiting longer, I was grateful that he still wanted to see me. It was a small reassurance, but it made me feel better. So, I carried on with my work, which I enjoyed, especially the social aspect of it. I had a good relationship with Cole, and I liked working with him. During our breaks, I would often go behind the garage to the supermarket car park to ride Cole's motorbike and have a fag. I talked to him about my relationship with Dan, and he mentioned that he'd like to have a girlfriend too. His words made me feel a bit sad for him, but it was nice to have someone to talk to.

At the end of the night, Cole bought the fags and grinned, saying, "Come on then, tell me the gossip." I laughed, and he asked, "Have you seen him yet? Do you miss him?"

"Yes, I do miss him," I admitted, "but I'm seeing him Friday."

Cole raised an eyebrow. "Why not tonight?"

"He's out with his friends," I replied, quickly changing the subject. I already felt a little insecure about not seeing him that evening, and I didn't need Cole making it worse. I climbed onto his bike and started laughing. I'd got used to nicking his bike and riding it around the car park. I'd never had a friend like Cole before, a boy I could trust and not fancy. It made everything feel easy, with no expectations, none of the awkwardness I'd usually feel around other lads.

To be honest, all we ever did was have a fag, mess about, and I'd dream about having a bike of my own. We talked about college and life in general, though in all the time I'd known him, Cole had never really shared much about his personal life. I'd never asked either; I figured if he wanted to tell me, he would. I knew he went to college and that was about it. Still, we chatted about all sorts. People who came into the garage, bits of gossip he'd heard, the usual everyday things. He did once open up about wanting a girlfriend, and I suppose he felt safe with me in the same way I felt safe with him. It was what you'd call a proper friendship, nothing complicated, just easy company.

After finishing our fag, we sat on the wall for a bit, chatting, until Cole said, "I've got to go now, I'll see you Friday."

"Yeah," I said as he left, and I wandered off towards home.

But as I got closer, I realised I didn't feel like going in. I still had this restless, unsettled feeling. So, on a bit of a whim, I decided to call for a girl from school. She lived nearby, but I'd never actually called for her before. Her house was a bungalow, like my parents', only it was on the main road. It looked small and run-down. The outside was grey brickwork, tired and uninviting, and there was a little porch that somehow made it seem colder. I think part of that feeling came from my own anxiety; turning up out of the blue without warning made me nervous. As I rang the bell, I wondered if she'd even want to see me. I stood there awkwardly, waiting. It felt like ages, and it was getting late. I turned to leave, already feeling foolish for having come, when the front door opened behind me.

A man's voice called out, "Can I help you?" and my stomach flipped a little with nerves.

Then Paula appeared at the door, recognising me straight away and telling him it was Mandy calling for her. She gave me a warm smile and quickly brought me inside, and somehow the hallway felt a lot less eerie with her there. She led me into her bedroom, and I flopped down onto the bed while she shut the door.

"I just didn't feel like going home yet," I said. "I wanted to tell someone my news and I thought you might want to know."

Paula wasn't exactly my best friend, but it felt right to tell her about what had been happening over the past couple of weeks. I mentioned that I had a boyfriend, and when she asked his name, I told her. Straight away, she said her friend had been with him, that they'd been engaged, and she'd ended it because Dan had become violent. I didn't want to hear this. It didn't fit with the story I was building in my head, the excitement of having a boyfriend again, and the sense of things finally looking up for me. I smiled politely, had a cup of tea, and soon after wanted to head home. The conversation hadn't gone how I'd hoped. I had been excited to share my news, but instead Paula seemed to know more about my new boyfriend than I did, and it left me feeling uneasy. I tried to clear my head, telling myself she might not know the full story. Besides, I didn't think much of the girl Paula claimed was his ex, so I convinced myself it might not even be true.

I went home afterwards and headed straight to bed, not feeling that great. I pushed the washing off the bed and climbed in, closing my eyes. A little while later, Mum came into the room, sat on the edge of the bed and asked, "Are you okay? You haven't come in to say hello and your dinner's still in the oven."

I looked up and said, "Oh, I forgot." As I said it, I realised I was actually starting to feel hungry. There was a warmth in her voice, a kind of love I didn't feel that often. Since I'd started this job, it felt like she missed me more. It was strange, but in a nice way. I told her I'd get up and have some dinner. Truth be told, I'd gone to bed because I was tired, but it was probably because I was hungry too. I didn't want her knowing about what Paula had said about Dan about him not wanting his name ruined or about my first proper boyfriend in ages coming to an end before it had properly begun.

I asked what dinner was and she said, "Shepherd's pie and vegetables."

Yum, I thought. I loved that. To be honest, I loved all Mum's cooking. She was the best cook, and I hoped to be a good cook like her one day, though she never let me in the kitchen to learn. I was so clueless, I didn't even know how a potato turned into mashed potato.

I made my way into the kitchen, took my dinner out of the oven and popped it in the microwave. I asked if there was any gravy, even though I didn't usually like it, but it made the vegetables easier to eat. I pulled the plate out of the microwave a little too quickly and dropped it as it burnt my hand. It banged against the worktop and Mum called from the lounge, "All okay?" without even getting up to check.

I grumbled, "Yeah, burnt my hand, but it's fine."

"Be careful," she replied.

I sat down with my knife and fork and tried the first bite carefully, it was still lukewarm, which surprised me, seeing as the plate had been scorching. It was as if the plate had cooked more than the food itself. I wanted to heat it up again but didn't fancy making the plate even hotter or annoying Mum. So I ate it like that. The vegetables were a bit warmer, and the gravy tasted surprisingly sweet, even though it was barely warm. I finished it quickly, feeling stuffed by the end, and my stomach ached.

I didn't feel like going straight back to bed, not with that bloated feeling, so I went and sat in the lounge with my parents, something I didn't usually do. Dad was quiet, as usual, and Mum was glued to the telly. I sat there, wanting to tell them about my day, knowing full well they wouldn't be interested, and Dad would probably get cross if I started rambling on. I got up, made myself a cup of tea, and headed back to my room. It felt better than sitting there being ignored.

I climbed into bed again, properly this time, undressed and lay there, closing my eyes. I thought about Dan, imagining us getting married, me not feeling so alone anymore. My eldest sister had a baby recently, and she was getting cuter by the day. It was nice having a baby around. There was a lot of attention on my sister at the moment, and Mum and Dad kept buying teddies and little things. I suppose that's what grandparents do. I was spending less time with my sister now, though. Mum had taken over, visiting her loads, and she and her husband came around often. I didn't mind, but I hardly got a look in when they were there. I woke in the night needing the toilet, but I couldn't see what time it was. I didn't have work tomorrow, and I was already dreading the day ahead, knowing it would drag. I was waiting to see Dan and it felt like ages away. I couldn't see Laura either because she was still at school; she was a year below me.

I knew I needed to clean Smokey out too. Dad had moved his run onto the concrete because his nails were getting long and, no surprise, Dad wasn't about to pay a vet to trim them. I wasn't the best at looking after the rabbit, if I'm honest. I hadn't cleaned him out in weeks, though Dad had probably done it for me at some point. He'd mentioned it yesterday and I hadn't hung about, not because I'm keen on chores but because I didn't fancy the consequences. Dad rarely did much in the way of actual punishment, but he ruled the house with the fear of what he could do. We were all too scared to test him. I got up, made another cup of tea and thought about sorting the rabbit out, then realised we'd run out of straw. That meant I'd have to go to the fruit and veg shop to get some. At least it gave me something to do, even if it was only walking up the road. I shoved my shoes on, headed out, and halfway down the road realised I hadn't picked up any money. I sighed and trudged back home. I'd lost all motivation by then but carried on anyway; I didn't have much choice.

I quickened my pace a little, and as I reached the end of the road, I spotted a neighbour. They were someone my parents knew better than I did, but I chatted with them anyway. The conversation was safe and predictable; they talked about the weather, complaining that it had been far too hot lately. I hadn't really noticed the heat much myself; perhaps it was an old person's thing, I thought, as I nodded and agreed just to keep the conversation moving. I'd always been good at chatting about nothing. It felt a little strange to me, even superficial, and I never quite understood why adults did it so often. When I went to the supermarket with my mum, she'd sometimes call me over quickly, almost as if to avoid speaking to people, but me, I would just chatter away aimlessly. At least it took my mind off walking. They asked where I was off to, so I explained I needed to fetch some straw to change the bunnies' bedding. When they asked where I'd be getting it from, I told them the fruit and veg shop sold straw. They were surprised by this and said how handy it was, to which I nodded, already feeling bored with the conversation. I was itching to get moving again, so I politely said, "Well, I'd better go now, bye." They said their goodbyes, and I hurried off, almost breaking into a sprint to put some distance between us and ease the awkwardness.

When I arrived at the shop, I immediately spotted the straw and picked it up. Just then, my friend's mother walked in behind me and began chatting. I felt a wave of frustration. All I wanted was to complete this one simple task. I had already forgotten the straw once, then the money, and now I was being drawn into conversation. The thought of exchanging polite, meaningless words was unbearable, especially when, deep down, I doubted anyone truly wished to engage in small talk either. However, since it was Laura's mum, I felt more obliged to be polite; at least I knew her, unlike the neighbours. Thankfully, she seemed to be in a hurry and quickly said she couldn't stop before heading off. Phew, that was easy, I thought to myself.

When I looked up, to my dismay, a queue had formed. There were now at least four people ahead of me, even though the shop had been empty before she started talking. I waited patiently, and soon enough, it was my turn. I paid, grabbed the straw, and hurried out before anyone else could stop me. As I walked home, I kept my gaze fixed to the ground, avoiding eye contact to escape the need for further greetings. I believed that if I didn't see them, I wasn't obliged to say anything. I was nearly home, at the top of my road, when I spotted my dad. That was the one person I didn't want to bump into; I still hadn't sorted the rabbit's bedding. But Dad looked pleased to see me. He asked what I was doing, and I told him I had just been to get straw for the rabbit. His face lit up with a big smile, and he said, "Good girl," which made me feel unexpectedly warm and content. When we got home, I went straight to the garden to change the rabbit's bedding. That's when I noticed he had started digging into the concrete, though I reasoned it had at least helped wear down his nails. With that task finally done, Dad called out from the door, asking if I wanted some lunch. I hadn't eaten all day and hadn't even thought about food until that moment, but suddenly I felt starving. I asked what he was making, and he suggested cheese on toast. I eagerly agreed. It was odd because I never particularly fancied cheese on toast, yet every time I had it, it tasted far better than I expected. I'd always tell myself I'd have it again the next day, though I never did.

It was Thursday, and I didn't have work that evening, which left me feeling restless and a little disappointed. I would have preferred to be busy rather than sitting at home. So, I called for Laura, and she was in. We went out together, wandering the streets as usual, sneaking into alleyways for a cigarette before walking around the block and back to her bungalow. She only lived about a mile and a half away, which was convenient, and we probably covered quite a distance with our wandering. Back at hers, we fell into our usual routine, making silly dance videos, pretending to sing and act like fools. Even though I was sixteen, I still found comfort in being silly. It helped me forget everything else. Laura was easy-going and never judged me. I felt truly safe around her, like she was a sister. In fact, I loved her deeply. I spent more time with her than with my own family. She was my cousin, best friend, and family all rolled into one. I often wondered how I would have coped with life without her. She was my anchor; being with her made me feel more stable, offering an escape from the house and the dark thoughts that sometimes haunted me.

Those thoughts would swirl around my head, leaving me feeling dirty and ashamed. I would think about my nanny and wonder what was wrong with her and why my grandad wouldn't just direct his attention towards her instead. It was strange. When it happened, I would always lie beside her at first, then she would tell me to move into the middle. At that moment, my stomach would lurch and a wave of fear would pass through me. My throat would dry, and I would feel powerless and voiceless. I would shut my eyes tightly and pretend to sleep. I would lie there, motionless, for what felt like an eternity, trying to judge whether it was safe, but inevitably it would begin. I dreaded hearing those words: "I know you're awake." The battle was lost then. The ordeal would unfold, and its trauma would settle into my soul, lingering long after morning arrived. Then the charade would begin again, pretending it never happened, with everyone playing happy families, wearing smiles and polite faces until I went home.

Chapter 9: Small Victories

Once those thoughts took hold, they would bring with them uncomfortable sensations, like the feeling of countless spiders crawling over my private parts. I would be gripped by an overwhelming urge to rub the feeling away, to erase the touch, to halt the invasion. The only way to escape those thoughts was by creating new ones, imagining being rescued and taken far away from it all. I had grown very skilled at dreaming, and always it was a man who came to save me. For weeks, the same dream played out in my mind. I would be standing in a field, like an army barracks, and a soldier would be walking towards me. As he drew closer, he would start to fade away. Just as our hands touched, I would wake up. I had this dream for months, and every time it left me with a deep sadness. I wanted to stay with him. His touch felt safe, warm, and reassuring; then he would disappear.

Being at Laura's always helped to stop the thoughts and made me feel good. It was a real comfort, because when I was with her, it felt like I was free from everything bad in my life. Her mum had a few boyfriends and Laura was often quite lonely, so in a way, we gave each other what we both needed. It just made sense. It was getting late though, and I needed to head home. Laura walked halfway with me, and we shared a fag before parting ways yet again. I was starting to feel the cold; I'd only put on a pair of shorts, and it was surprisingly chilly for a July evening. I tried to pick up my pace to warm myself up, but it didn't do much. Just then, I heard a car horn beep. I looked up to see Dan and his mates in a car. He had a huge smile on his face, and it made me so happy to see him. I was nearly at the end of my road, and suddenly I didn't feel as cold anymore. Seeing Dan made everything feel a little better, and I didn't mind the chill because I knew I'd be seeing him tomorrow, and it was clear from his smile that he was happy to see me too.

When I got home, the house was empty. I made myself a drink and wondered what would be for dinner. It was quite late, so I checked the microwave to see if my dinner had been left in there, but it wasn't. I then looked in the oven and found it: a plate of pork chops, roast potatoes, and vegetables, with a small pot of gravy on the side. It looked delicious. I lifted the gravy and placed it in the microwave to heat through. I was about to do the same with the dinner but realised it was still reasonably warm. Besides, I didn't much like pork chops reheated, as they tended to dry out too much, and the potatoes lost their crispiness.

I made sure the gravy was piping hot, intending to pour it over everything to soak into the meat and vegetables. My mouth was watering as I waited. Just as I was about to eat, I felt the urgent need to use the toilet, so I left the dinner warming while I went. Unfortunately, once in the bathroom, I discovered there was no toilet paper on the holder. I had no choice but to shuffle awkwardly into the hallway with my shorts around my ankles, hoping no one would arrive home and catch me. Urine dribbled down my leg as I hurried to the airing cupboard where Mum kept the toilet rolls. I nearly tripped over my shorts but managed to grab a roll and make it back without incident, although with a little mishap down my legs, but at least the task was done. After cleaning up and pulling my shorts back on, I washed my hands but couldn't be bothered to replace the roll on the holder, so I left it balanced on top of the cistern. That was the extent of my effort for the evening.

I returned to the kitchen just as the front door opened. I thought to myself, phew, I nearly got caught, and chuckled quietly. I sat down to eat my dinner, which, to my delight, was as good as if Mum had just served it up herself. I mashed one of the potatoes into the vegetables to make them taste better, then ate the vegetables first. I always saved the best part of the meal for last so that the nicest flavour would linger in my mouth after I finished eating. To me, this made perfect sense. My mum, however, always ate her favourite part first and rarely touched her vegetables. In many ways, she was like a little girl.

That evening, I didn't feel like being around anyone. As usual, I offered my parents a cup of tea, made mine, and then quietly disappeared into my bedroom. I climbed into bed and allowed myself to drift into daydreams, which helped pass the time. By the time I finished my tea, I was already half-asleep. The following day was Friday. I woke up late, feeling lively and full of anticipation because I was seeing Dan after work. It was already close to midday, so I got up, made myself a cup of tea, and had a rather uninspiring lunch, Weetabix with jam. It was dry, but Mum hadn't done the shopping, and as she often said, beggars can't be choosers. I ate it without complaint. After lunch, I went for a walk. The afternoon passed quickly, and before long it was time for work. I felt as though everything was a rush again, even though I hadn't done much all day.

As I was leaving my close, I saw my brother walking towards me, eating jam doughnuts, my favourite. We were alike in that neither of us cared for cream cakes. Whenever Mum treated us to something from the bakery, we always chose jam doughnuts, and she would buy us two each. This time, my brother had an entire bag to himself. I asked if I could have one, but he told me to get lost. He then shoved a whole doughnut into his mouth and, grinning, said, "Yum," as he walked past. Typical brotherly behaviour, I thought. He had at least six in the bag; what harm would it have done to give me one? Still, I soon forgot about it as I drew closer to work, my excitement building at the thought of seeing Dan later.

Work always passed quickly when I was with Cole, and to be honest, I enjoyed his company so much that I wasn't even thinking about Dan until afterwards. As I turned the corner into work, I spotted Cole already on the forecourt, grinning as he filled up a customer's car. I asked what he was doing there so early, and he explained that he hadn't had college that day and had been asked to come in early. I felt a flicker of annoyance, thinking that if I'd known, I would have gone in earlier too, even without pay. That, to me, was the mark of a real friend, wanting to be around someone simply for their company. What I valued most about my friendship with Cole was that there was no physical contact, no unspoken expectations. It felt good to be liked for who I was, rather than what someone could take from me. I was also relieved to see that Cole had ended up serving the bloke who always made me uncomfortable, the one who stared at my bum while I filled his car. The thought of being spared that made a small smile spread across my face.

I walked into the shop and saw Daniel, the boss, standing there. I said hello, and he seemed in a particularly chatty mood, feeling good about life. He talked for about half an hour, which was a little unusual, but I never questioned it. Cole, on the other hand, looked thoroughly bored, clearly wishing Daniel would leave. As soon as Daniel walked out, Cole muttered, "Thank God for that boring bastard."

I didn't mind Daniel. I actually thought he was quite nice. I looked up to him in a way, admired his business and his Mercedes. He seemed alright to me, and I really liked Denise, who worked upstairs as well. I suspected Daniel liked Denise a little more than he probably should, considering he was married, and so was she, but it wasn't my business. I didn't give much thought to things like that. My world had far too much else going on to worry about such things. I liked them both and didn't judge. I turned to Cole and said, "Don't be mean." He grinned and replied, "I've been dying to find out more about you and lover boy." I pulled a face and shrugged. "Nothing to say; I haven't seen him. Well, I waved to him yesterday, but that's it."

Cole tutted and joked, "That's the highlight of my life currently." I laughed and said, "What shall we do then? I've got a cousin, Laura, fancy a date with her?" Cole's face lit up at the idea. "Yes, please."

I cringed slightly inside, knowing that while Cole was my friend and a lovely lad, I'd never had any real feelings for him. I wondered if I was doing Laura a bit of a disservice by even suggesting it. But my loyalty to Cole made it worth a shot. He might not have been handsome, but he was a genuinely nice boy.

I said, "Okay, I'll sort it out; leave it to me." Just then, a bloke walked in and, in a very stern voice, asked, "Is anyone actually serving today?" Cole's eyes went wide, and he gave me this awkward little smile before hurrying out the door. I was relieved, to be honest, I didn't fancy serving someone in a foul mood. I had enough of dodging moods at home; I didn't need to deal with it at work too. Most of our customers were lovely, and he was the only one since I'd started there who'd come in cross. I supposed that wasn't bad in the grand scheme of things.

I looked out to where Cole was and saw him standing there, looking completely unbothered. He didn't seem to care about the man. By the time Cole came back in, the bloke had driven off; he must have paid him quickly and left without needing a receipt.

Curious, I asked Cole, "What did he say?" half expecting him to tell me off or complain.

But Cole shrugged and said, "He was actually alright. Said sorry about being short, he was just off out, didn't see anyone about, and didn't have time to find another garage tonight."

I smiled and said, "I didn't even see his car pull up. Did you?"

Cole let out a laugh and said, "I thought I saw something, but we were chatting, and I sort of forgot about it."

I told him it was his turn to make the tea and asked where Daniel had got to. He reckoned Daniel had gone upstairs. Then I said, "Fancy a chocolate bar?" and we helped ourselves without putting it on the tab, although with what we were paid, I figured it balanced out somewhere. I had a Mars bar, Cole went for a Double Decker, and I grabbed a packet of crisps too, but I did put those on the tab. I wasn't too greedy. Most of the time, I added things to my tab, but sometimes I didn't, just for the thrill of it, knowing I wasn't really supposed to. Not that I needed the money. I used to put it all in a drawer at home. It was about half full now. Every time I got paid, I handed my parents their share, and the rest just went into that drawer. It wasn't much these days since I had to pay rent, eight pounds out of my nineteen and once my tab was cleared, I was left with seven or eight pounds. But I didn't mind. What did I need money for? I wasn't into fashion. I didn't care much for music either. We didn't have a stereo until I was fifteen, and by then, I'd got used to not being the popular one who knew all the songs and bands.

I was just me, minimalistic and boring, probably. But I was alright with it. I liked my new working life. It got me away from home. Though the pressure was mounting back there. Now that I was out of school and only had a part-time job, I was being pushed to either go full-time at the garage or sign up for a youth training scheme. Neither appealed to me, and for now, I was dodging the conversation, sneaking out whenever I could to avoid it.

I didn't know what I wanted to do, and it still stung that Mum wouldn't let me go to college. Whenever I tried to think about my future, the old fears crept in, that I'd be useless, not clever enough, that no one would like me. The same things that haunted me any time I had to face something new.

Chapter 10: Love Without

Conditions

I liked working with Cole. After we finished work, we always went out for a fag. We didn't even ask each other anymore; it was just a given. One evening, while we were standing out there, I asked him what he planned to do after college. He didn't know. I could tell he didn't want to talk about it either. And because I'd been in that same place, I wasn't about to push him. So, I quickly changed the subject.

"Can I have your keys and take your bike for a spin round the car park?" I asked.

He laughed, "You love riding that bike, don't you?"

I nodded and laughed too.

"Why don't you get one? You could get a job most places then," he said.

"Maybe," I replied, though deep down, I knew it probably wouldn't happen. I felt comfy then, happy for a moment. But suddenly, it hit me; I swore and stopped dead.

"Oh my God! I've got to go; I completely forgot Dan's coming round. Shit, I need to get home!"

Cole's face shifted and he said, "Oh yeah, I'm sorry; I forgot too." He looked properly guilty, like he felt he should have reminded me. But I was already moving, sprinting off, my heart pounding. I didn't have a watch and had no idea what time it was. I finished at eight and couldn't have been with Cole too long after. It was probably half past eight by now. I was panicking, wondering if Dan had come round and whether Mum would have invited him in or sent him away. The worst part was, I didn't even know where he lived. I remembered him saying it was somewhere in Hythe, but he'd never told me the address.

I ran as fast as I could, my throat burning, not just from running but from the anxiety squeezing my chest. I turned the corner to our road, and the sight of no car in the drive made my stomach drop. I opened the front door; no one was home. I went straight to the kitchen and flicked the kettle on, feeling heavy with disappointment. I've missed him, I thought miserably. And then, the doorbell rang. My heart leapt to my throat, my stomach turning somersaults as I crossed the hall. I held my breath, hoping with everything I had that it was Dan. And there he was. All six foot four of him, standing awkwardly in the porch. Tall and thin, but I didn't care about that. He had to duck to get in. I smiled, and he walked in without waiting for me to say anything.

He grabbed me, pulled me close, and said, "I've missed you."

His lips met mine, and our tongues touched, reacquainting themselves with the feeling they'd known just a week before. That horrible knot in my stomach loosened, and I stretched up onto my tiptoes, wrapping my arms

120

around his neck, straining as far as I could to reach him. He bent slightly, meeting me halfway. It felt nice having to stretch, reaching up to meet him, my whole body pulling towards that kiss. His hands rested on my bum, squeezing gently, then moved up to the small of my back. I squirmed. A shiver raced down my spine, and a strange, electric sort of feeling shot through me, making me squirm again.

I led him into the lounge and we settled down for a while before I went to make him a cup of tea. He followed me into the kitchen, and as I stood facing the kettle, he began gently rubbing my back. I felt that familiar, warm sensation in my stomach, a fluttering, almost delicious feeling, and instinctively, I pressed my bum against him and also rubbed myself down on him. I liked the way it made me feel. I wanted so much to turn around and face him, but as I went to move, he held me in place and whispered softly in my ear, "Oh no you don't; you are making the tea remember." I felt myself going weaker at the knees and I had an excited feeling I had never experienced before and I didn't want it to stop. It was fairly innocent yet all-encompassing and I felt horny. I could feel myself becoming wet. I wanted him. I felt the need more and more to kiss him and because somehow, the way he was putting off the moment it felt more and more arousing. He was making me giggle and this seemed to make him more aroused as I could feel him pushing into my back. But then, quite suddenly, a wave of fear crept in. My excitement turned to unease, my mouth grew dry, and my throat tightened. I stiffened slightly, and he noticed at once. Without needing to speak, he seemed to understand,

121

stepping back gently. He placed a light kiss on my cheek and said with a knowing smile, "Is the tea ready yet?"

I felt a quiet relief that my feelings and the moment remained unspoken, giving me space to gather myself. I turned away to drop the used teabag into the bin, then picked up the cups and made my way back into the lounge.

We were chatting, laughing, and playfully poking each other, and it felt as though time had been put on fast forward. I knew he would have to go home soon, and I felt a pang of sadness at the thought. I heard the door and wondered whether Dad was on nights or if he might be coming in with Mum. My heart sank a little.

I was relieved when Mum walked into the room on her own. I looked up and said, "Oh, Dan came round." She smiled and replied, "Oh, okay, nice to see you, Dan." He held out his hand to greet her, and she asked, "Where are you staying tonight? It's getting late." Dan stuttered a little, "Oh, I'll be off home soon," as though he'd taken her words as a polite hint to leave. To our surprise, Mum added, "You're welcome to stay on the couch; it's late. Ken will be in from nights, but I don't think he'll disturb you."

I felt a wave of apprehension at the thought of Dad walking in and having a go at Dan. When I voiced my anxiety, Mum reassured me, "If he finds you together, he'll be cross, but if Dan's just on the sofa, it'll be fine." I smiled gratefully. Dan then politely declined, "I'll walk home tonight, but thank you; it was kind of you to offer." He explained that he needed to do his washing, go to the launderette and do some shopping, offering Mum a polite smile as she, already distracted, hummed to herself and wandered out of the room.

A moment later, Dan sighed, "Actually, I should get going," before leaning over to kiss me again. This time, I felt more at ease, my mind clearer, and my body relaxed. I felt myself responding to him, wishing he could stay. I wanted to be close to him, to feel his warmth and let our bodies entwine. As those thoughts flickered in my mind, he stood up and reached for my hand, gently pulling me from the sofa.

"I'll come back tomorrow after I've done my chores," he grinned. I laughed, "You sound like an old man," then shuddered at the uninvited thought and brushed it away. Holding him felt comforting and so natural, like something I hadn't known before. It wasn't a familiar feeling in my life, but it was good. I didn't want him to go, but him telling me he'd come back made it easier, like he felt the same about leaving.

As he led me to the front door, I was struck again by how tall he was and how safe it felt to lean into him. Just before opening the door, he turned, pulled me into his arms, and pressed his face against mine. He seemed to sense my every move, reading my body, knowing what I needed without a word. I pulled back, needing to see his face. My hands cupped his cheeks, and I drew him in, our lips meeting again. My fingers wove through his hair as I invited his tongue to meet mine. It was as though our tongues were old friends reunited after a long absence, moving together naturally, their size and pace in perfect harmony. There was a warmth, a connection, and the kiss lingered, not too much, just enough.

I felt his hands on my hips again, squeezing slightly before pulling away and giving my bottom a playful slap. "Enough of this," he murmured with a grin, "or I'll never go home."

I didn't want him to leave. I longed to feel his body against mine, to fall asleep in his arms. My mouth already missed his kiss. I groaned softly and reached up for one final lingering embrace, our tongues meeting one last time before parting naturally as we both came up for air. Smiling, he said, "Right, I'm going. I'll call by tomorrow; we can chill in your garden if it's sunny."

I nodded, "Okay," and watched as he left, walking up the path. I closed the door behind him. Skipping my usual cup of tea, I headed straight to the bathroom, brushed my teeth, and went to bed.

Sleep came quickly; it had been an eventful evening and I was exhausted. I wasn't quite sure what had happened between us, but Dan's easy going nature had kept me from overthinking it at the time. It was only after he'd gone that my thoughts turned chaotic. I let them swirl in my mind before doing what I'd always done, suppressing them, letting the other feelings take over. I'd enjoyed his company so much and loved seeing him again. But the thought of eventually having sex with him was starting to weigh on me. It felt scary, especially knowing he had his own flat. I wasn't even sure why; I just felt confused and uneasy. I dwelled on it as I made my way to the kitchen, craving a cup of tea. But to my surprise, the room was crowded, my aunty and uncle had arrived, and I hadn't heard a thing. Their loud, excited voices filled the house. I did the obligatory greetings, offering quick kisses on cheeks, feeling awkward as I played the dutiful daughter while wishing I could disappear. I realised I wasn't even wearing proper bottoms, just my knickers. Dad, in typical fashion, shouted, "Go and get some clothes on, will you!" It was, oddly, a relief. It gave me the perfect excuse to grab my tea and retreat to my room, with no intention of going back out there again.

I finished my tea and then got dressed, wondering if my aunt and uncle were still there, as the house had fallen unusually quiet. The bungalow seemed oddly soundproof, because the moment I opened my bedroom door again, I could hear the familiar murmur of voices. I felt a little more welcome this time, perhaps because I was now dressed. I'd chosen my blue shorts; they were looser than most of my other clothes, which I preferred. I couldn't stand the feeling of fabric pressing against my crotch; it gave me an awful, crawling sensation, like a thousand tiny spiders brushing against my skin. To avoid this, I always opted for looser, more comfortable clothes, and today, those blue shorts were my safest choice. I hadn't noticed how quickly time had passed. Glancing up at the clock, I saw it was already two o'clock. I began to wonder what time Dan might turn up. Part of me wasn't sure I wanted him around at the moment, with everything that had been going on, but another part of me missed him. The thought made me smile to myself. Just then, Dad called out, "You alright?" and I nodded in reply before stepping out of the room.

Just as I turned around, the doorbell rang. I ran to answer it, praying it was Dan, and it was. I opened the door and said, "It's a madhouse in here today." He smiled and bent down to place a kiss on my forehead. Then, as if to say "let me meet this mad bunch", he gestured for me to lead the way. For some reason, I felt shy, but I guided him into the lounge where everyone was gathered, chatting away. Mum had even been to the shops and bought treats, a rare occurrence in our house. Normally, when treats did appear, it was a free-for-all. We'd scoff the lot until we felt sick and it was all gone. I suppose it was because we hardly ever had them, so when we did, it became a race to get your share, since you never knew when the next lot would come along. I smiled to myself, happy that Dan might think it was normal for us to have treats like that. I asked Mum if Dan could have a cake and, playing the gracious host, she replied, "Of course," as if she were the most generous lady alive. It was one of those games we played, pretending that life was always like this, full of treats and laughter. I didn't mind those games, though; they were the good times, rare as they were, and I made the most of them.

Dan helped himself to a French Fancy and I joined him. I always went for the lemon one because it actually tasted of lemon. The others barely tasted of anything, and I really disliked chocolate-flavoured things. I liked proper chocolate, but there was something about chocolate flavouring I could always tell apart. Though even proper chocolate didn't much like me. It gave me spots, made my stomach bloat, left me feeling lethargic and unwell, and made going to the toilet painful. Yet I still ate it sometimes because, in that moment, it felt good. I had stopped eating it for a year when the acne was at its worst, but it eventually calmed down.

I spotted the empty garden through the window, grabbed Dan's hand and suggested we sit outside. I led him through to the back where the garden wrapped around the bungalow. Mum was a keen gardener, and the borders were always colourful and bright. I felt proud showing him the blooms. The reclining chairs were out, a real privilege, as they belonged to my parents, and I wouldn't have had a chance if they'd been in the garden. Thankfully, they weren't. The chairs sat under the big tree where Mum used to sunbathe with no top on. She liked the shade too, so the recliners stayed there.

I would have preferred to sit out in the full sun, but I wasn't about to move the chairs. The last thing I wanted was for my parents to reveal their true colours while Dan was here. I wasn't taking any risks.

The whole scene reminded me of a time when my best friend stayed over. We were having a good evening in the lounge with Dad. He was in a decent mood until, out of nowhere, he snapped and told us to go to bed. At first, I laughed, thinking he was joking, but then his face twisted with anger. He took off his watch and hurled it at me, hitting me hard on the head. I sat there, stunned, unsure how to react; my friend was right there, and I could see how scared and awkward she felt. I was mortified. I reached out to touch her hand, trying to reassure her, and quickly ushered her out of the room.

That was Dad for you. He could go from calm to furious in a heartbeat. I could never read him; it was always unpredictable. Fortunately, my friend never mentioned it afterwards. We just went to bed, both unusually quiet. I think she probably didn't know what to say, and maybe she felt sorry for me, though I never wanted anyone's pity. I'd play pretend games in my head, imagining a normal life. Lorna, my friend, had confided in me too. Her dad was much older than her mum and a bit odd. She once told me how he'd called her a tart, and never one to back down, she'd snapped back, "Why don't you come up and see me sometime?" That really set him off, and he'd slapped her hard across the face. She told me she gave him a look of pure disgust and walked out. Lorna had often been unhappy at school and had her own troubles. That's why, with Dan around, I was determined to avoid anything remotely risky. I couldn't bear the thought of him seeing any of that side of my family; it might put him off me.

I offered him a drink and headed indoors to fetch it. He didn't follow, as though he could sense it was best to stay put. He always seemed to get the measure of a situation. Inside, I quickly popped my head into the lounge to ask Mum and Dad if it was alright for us to use the recliners while Dan was outside. They were in a good mood, showing off for company, so the answer was a cheerful "Yes, of course!" Relief washed over me. Now I could relax, knowing I wouldn't have to worry about them making a fuss.

The kettle had just boiled, so I got two cups out when Dad shouted, "I hope you're making tea for all of us!" I wasn't about to say no. "Yes, of course," I called back, sighing under my breath. This was turning into a major operation. I realised I'd have to boil the kettle a second time for me and Dan. I poured water into the teapot for them, refilled the kettle, and rummaged for the tray. I loaded everything onto it, but the milk jug was nowhere to be seen. I started to worry, conscious of how long Dan had been left alone in a strange garden.

I called out to Mum, asking where the milk jug was. "Probably right in front of your face, knowing you," she teased. My stomach sank. I didn't like the sound of this; it was her favourite party trick to poke fun at me in front of guests. I cringed, silently pleading, please, not today, Mum. Not with Dan here. As if by magic, she appeared, went straight to the cupboard, and handed me the milk jug. I quickly filled it and added it to the tray. Carrying it into the lounge, I set it down on the small coffee table and left the room, eager to get back outside before anything else could go wrong.

The kettle had boiled again, and now I needed to wash two mugs, one for me and one for Dan, before making the tea. I wondered what he might say, as I'd been ages. But when I stepped out into the garden, it struck me as odd in a lovely sort of way. There he was, stretched out on the recliner with his eyes closed, looking completely relaxed, as though he hadn't even noticed how long I'd been gone. It pleased me more than I cared to admit. I leaned over him for a moment, casting a shadow and blocking out the sun. He opened one eye, grinned, and said, "Oi, you're ruining my tan!" and laughed. I smiled and apologised, explaining that I'd had to make tea for everyone first. He chuckled and said he'd cleverly avoided that job by choosing to sunbathe while I played hostess. I gave him a playful shove and said, "Oh, thanks for that!" It felt nice; he seemed so at ease, like he genuinely enjoyed being in our garden. I liked that he didn't seem remotely bothered by all the people around.

I lay down beside him and closed my eyes. The sun was intensely hot on my face, and beads of sweat gathered on the side of my nose. I hadn't been sitting there for more than five minutes before I began to feel too hot. Picking up my recliner, I wheeled it into the shade.

Dan looked over and said, "Oh, you're leaving me?"

"Never," I replied with a smile.

"Come here," he said.

"Why?" I asked, playing along.

"Because I want to cuddle you," he answered.

I laughed and teased, "Come and get me then."

Without hesitation, he jumped up and ran over, grabbing me and collapsing onto the bed beside me. I couldn't stop giggling as he started kissing me, and we both tumbled into the recliner, our sides pressed against one another. It felt good, simple and easy, as if for a brief moment, everything was exactly as it should be.

We lay there quietly for a while, like he was searching for the right words. Then he said, "You should come to my flat soon."

I turned to look at him. I wasn't sure if he noticed the awkward flicker across my face, though I'd become quite good at hiding my true feelings. Part of me was desperate to go, to see his place, to know his surroundings and learn more about him. But there was another part, the darker, more fearful side of me, that felt insecure, haunted by possibilities I couldn't quite name. It was always the unknown that frightened me most. Oddly, when things actually happened, they were easier to deal with than the imagined fears beforehand. I agreed to go, realising it was inevitable, and told myself to remain calm.

He suggested waiting until next weekend so we could listen to the Top Ten on Sunday. I nodded like a shy child. I wasn't a virgin, but the thought of being intimate with someone new filled me with dread. When I'd been with Ryan, it had taken four months before we'd had sex. I knew things wouldn't be like that with Dan. He had his own flat. He was a grown-up. Ryan, though older, still lived with his mum. Dan's independence made him feel older, and the whole situation seemed scarier because of it.

It wasn't that I didn't want sex; in fact, I loved touching him and feeling him press against me, and I had felt desire. But it was the next step that scared me. Maybe it was because of the memories that came back whenever I stayed at Grandad's house. Staying there was always worse than when he came to my house. I never really understood why, but I tried not to dwell on those black thoughts, even though they lurked in the background, ready to consume me when I least expected it.

Chapter 11: The Strength in Forgiveness

The feelings from those times were impossible to fully explain. The best I could describe it was like having a million spiders crawling all over the private parts of my body, ravaging me, terrifying me to the point where I couldn't even speak. It was the only way I could find to put words to the helplessness I felt. I lost control, my rights, my dignity, and my voice. I became a vessel, something used.

Sometimes, I would escape in my mind, pretending it wasn't happening. If I concentrated hard enough, I could block it out. That worked until I needed the toilet. Then it would all come flooding back. The pain, oh, the pain, I knew it well. The burning sting of the first passing urine, the need to grip the walls, pushing and holding tight as I waited for the pain to fade. Eventually, the flow would ease, and with it, so would the sharpness of the pain, if only slightly.

Afterwards, I would block it out again. Pretend it hadn't happened. My mind couldn't properly process it anyway. It left me confused and lost. And most of all, betrayed by the very person who was supposed to protect me. A grandfather. A family figure I should have loved.

Most children adore their grandad, I lost mine long before he physically died.

The man I truly loved, my gentle giant of a grandfather, passed away when I was twelve. That was traumatic for me, too. He never wanted to hurt me. The real him wouldn't have touched me or made me hold his penis.

A sudden nudge from Dan snapped me back to the present. I hadn't even realised how long I'd been lost in thought.

"Oi, you," I teased.

We started joking and laughing again, falling into each other's company like it was the easiest thing in the world. His hand found the small of my back, gently rubbing in slow circles, sending a shudder through me. I'd never felt anything quite like it before, though I realised I rather liked it, perhaps too much. The sun had grown even hotter since we first lay out there. It was now early afternoon, and the sun hung high in the sky, leaving little shade except for a small patch beneath the tree trunk, though I didn't care much for lying under the tree for long. I preferred the sun.

It struck me then how different things had been with Ryan. Though we dated, we never lay out like this together. We were always with friends, never alone. The only time I visited his family was when I bunked off school to go to his auntie's, and that had been difficult to manage. Still, to me, it had felt deep because it was my first relationship. I knew Ryan had been with other girls; one of them still hung around, and though she was older and they'd clearly had a proper relationship, I never saw her as a threat. I felt strangely secure about it.

I even liked Trudy, despite her being slightly unhinged. She was fun and probably still fancied Ryan, but I couldn't blame her. My sister knew her better than I did; she was older, and everyone knew everyone in our area. If you didn't know someone directly, you knew of them. And having three siblings meant I met plenty of people through their friends, especially my brothers' mates, which, truthfully, I didn't mind at all.

I'd already slept with a couple of boys, not because I wanted to, but because I needed to feel loved. As a child, I'd rarely felt that. They'd said the words often enough, but I would have much preferred to feel it rather than hear it. Even when they did love me, I often felt isolated and alone. I suppose that was Grandad's doing, and how it was handled.

Dan reached down to pick up his cup, nearly tipping me off the recliner in the process. The chair wobbled for a moment before settling back the right way, thank goodness. He grabbed his drink and grinned. "Go make me another, woman," he teased. I laughed and said, "Alright, are you hungry?" He nodded, so I headed into the lounge to grab some food. Mum had put out loads because we had company, and it felt like such a treat being able to help myself to the lovely spread.

Food was something that got eaten fast in our house, and my parents often ate after we'd gone to bed. Mornings before school, I'd walk downstairs and see empty wrappers scattered on the floor, evidence of the biscuits or sweets they'd devoured the night before. My mum didn't like her body image either, but I learned that in a way I wish I hadn't. It's not a memory I wanted to keep. When we lived in the guest house, I was desperate for something to eat, but asking for food wasn't easy. I knew I'd likely get shouted at, especially with Dad out. Still, I was starving, so I went looking for Mum. I checked everywhere, finally creeping toward her bedroom. The door was ajar. I peeked in, hoping she was there. What I saw froze me. My mind couldn't grasp it at first. Mum was on the bed, punching herself in the head, then her face, muttering, 'You're fat and ugly and horrible.' She yanked at her hair, her movements frantic. I didn't understand why she was doing it, but it scared me. I slipped away quickly, terrified she'd catch me watching. I knew she'd be furious if she found out I'd seen her like that. My stomach churned with pity and confusion, but I couldn't ask her about it. There was no explanation that felt safe. That memory lingered, surfacing now and then, making me uneasy. I never spoke of it, not until now, and it still feels raw to share. Those moments shaped how I saw her, a woman carrying her own pain, just as I carried mine.

Usually, I just got whatever was going, no questions asked. We never had much in the way of sweet things, and when it came to sandwiches, the fillings were awful; it was always jam or chocolate spread. Most times, I'd opt for toast with margarine instead. Today was different, though. There were sausage rolls, and Mum had made her famous quiche. Once you'd tasted her quiche, there was no going back; it was honestly like heaven. I often thought how lucky I was that she could cook. Imagine only having one food option and it being awful. I genuinely thanked my lucky stars when it came to her cooking. At least the meals I got at home were something to look forward to. Most of the time, I didn't eat much else besides the odd sweet or packet of crisps from the garage.

I loaded Dan's plate with all the things I knew he'd love and took it out to him while the kettle was boiling. I didn't think much about waiting on him; that's just how it was in my house. Men asked or shouted, and women did their duty. It felt normal to me. I'd even come to accept the idea that it was okay for a man to hit a woman, though the thought made me flinch.

For instance, one evening, when my parents and siblings were all out, Dan and I had the bungalow to ourselves. We were messing about, chatting, getting to know each other better. I opened up about my past, sharing things I rarely spoke of. I don't recall exactly what I said, but it must have hit a nerve. We were in my bedroom, Dan straddling me playfully, when his mood shifted. In an instant, he got furious, his fist raised toward my face before slamming into the wall beside me. Fear surged through me, cold and familiar. I'd seen my dad hit my mum countless times, but I'd always sworn no man would ever hit me. Yet here I was, frozen, telling myself Dan was 'nice' for hitting the wall instead of me. Deep down, I knew it was wrong. When my sister came home later, his hand was swollen, throbbing with pain. Her boyfriend took him to casualty to get it sorted. She pressed me about it, worried he'd been violent, but I denied it, insisting he was just messing about and it went wrong. I didn't want her to tell me to end things. Despite knowing it was a red flag, I was so desperate for love that I couldn't risk losing him. I felt disappointed in myself, but I'd grown up believing I was to blame for anger, just like when Dad said Mum deserved it for having the last word. I convinced myself I'd provoked Dan, that I'd said something wrong. We never spoke of it again, but it lingered, a warning I ignored. Looking back, I see the signs were there. Decisions we make can have long-lasting effects, not always bad, but far-reaching. I don't regret staying with Dan, for reasons I'll share in later books, but there's a lesson here: trust your gut. If I'd listened to my intuition, sharpened through meditation, I might have taken an easier path. Listen to the signs, they're there for a reason as you will come to learn later.

Back to our moment with Dan, I continued placed the plate on his lap, and he pulled me in for a massive kiss, thanking me with a big smile. "You chose well," he laughed, trying to stuff a sausage roll into my mouth. Then, grinning, he jumped up and started running. I grabbed another sausage roll and chased after him, shouting, "This one's for you, and it's going in your mouth the same way!" He was teasing, clearly in a playful mood, and I liked that about him. He didn't take life too seriously, and when he cuddled me, it felt genuine, not forced or false.

The sun was losing its warmth and the day was winding down. After finishing all the food, Dan sighed, "I suppose I better be getting back soon. Got to do my washing and the housework." My heart quickened at the thought of him leaving. I missed him already. When he was with me, the loneliness that usually lingered seemed to disappear, and I felt like I truly belonged somewhere. I grabbed him, cupping his head in my hands, running my fingers through his hair. "I'll see you tomorrow, I hope," I said softly. He pressed his lips to mine, a gentle, closed-mouth kiss that seemed to say, of course, and I knew what it meant. He was so tall, and I loved reaching up to him, standing on tiptoe. Strangely, that always turned me on, especially when it was time to say goodbye. Maybe it was my body's way of feeling safe, knowing he was leaving soon. Not that I meant to tease him, and he never mentioned it either.

Though my aunty and uncle were still there, and I hadn't seen them for a while, I couldn't help but feel sad about Dan going. We walked back inside, where everyone was gathered in the lounge. He said his goodbyes, and I followed him to the front porch so we could say our proper farewell. As I reached up, he instinctively lowered his head so I could wrap my hands around it, my favourite thing, massaging the back of his neck and feeling him lean into my touch. He pulled me closer, and I could feel the tension rising between us. I felt hot as he pressed against me, and I noticed him respond, his body shifting. I let my hands trail from his head to his shoulders, down his back; he was slender but had muscles beneath the surface. I ran my hands to his chest, slipped them under his shirt, feeling his skin, his nipples, until I reached the top of his jeans. Then, teasingly, I pulled away

"You wait till you're in my flat," he murmured, grinning. "Then we can carry this on."

I giggled and gave him one final kiss before he kissed my forehead and promised, "I'll see you tomorrow, after you've finished work."

I headed back into the lounge, where the evening passed quickly, and soon enough the week flew by too. Before I knew it, it was Friday again. Dan came round, and we decided to meet up with Mark and Lynn. It had only been a week, but as Dan spent most of his time with Mark, it felt like ages in his world. They picked us up at half nine, which felt late to me as I was usually in bed by ten. Lynn jumped out of the front seat to sit in the back with me, greeting me warmly. Though we'd only met recently, we got on well; no awkward silences, just easy conversation. She told me about her job and how work was stressing her out lately. I listened, though I'd only just left school and worked part-time at the garage.

Chapter 12: Finding Light

Within

Sometimes it bothered me, feeling young and a bit foolish compared to them, but I managed to brush it off most of the time. When we arrived at the pub, the lads went to get drinks, and Lynn and I found a seat by the window. It felt cosier there, tucked out of the way. The pub was bustling, and as we chatted, she asked what I'd been up to.

"Not a lot," I replied. "Although, I've got a bit of news."

"Oh yeah?" she asked, leaning in with interest. "Are you pregnant?"

I burst out laughing. "No! We haven't even had sex yet."

She chuckled. "Ah, immaculate conception, then!" I had no idea what that meant, but I laughed anyway, feeling a bit daft.

"Well, go on then," she grinned. "Tell me before the boys get back, what's this big secret?"

"I'm going to Dan's flat tomorrow," I said. "And, well... yeah, it might happen."

She threw her head back in laughter. "See? I wasn't far off with my guess."

I gulped. "I'm not getting pregnant though... I hope."

At that, we both cracked up laughing just as the boys appeared, asking what was so funny. We glanced at them, then at each other, and said in unison, "Private joke."

I smiled, knowing this was the start of a good friendship.

The four of us got on really well, and the boys loved making us laugh, almost as though they were competing to see who could be the funniest. Lynn didn't realise how well I knew Mark, but because I spent so much time with Dan, and Mark was always around, I'd got to know him too, long before we were actually dating. We all had a few drinks, though mine were non-alcoholic. I didn't mind, really. I'd never properly got into alcohol and didn't feel out of place without it. Every time I'd tried it, I'd found it disgusting, so I was quite happy sitting there with my orange juice, sipping it slowly because I rarely had a second. Even though the lads bought us our drinks, I never felt quite right about it because I didn't have any money on me. Well, actually, I did now, but I'd completely forgotten about it as it was tucked away in my drawer at home.

We had decided to call it a night and drove back to my parents' house. Dan said to drop him there too and gave me a smile. He came inside, and Mum offered him a blanket and the lounge again for the night, which he accepted. It made me feel warm inside. We spent the rest of the evening cuddling and kissing. At one point, I nearly drifted off before waking in a panic, realising I needed to go to bed. I knew if I fell asleep down there, my dad would be furious, and Dan would probably never be allowed to stay again. The thought terrified me. As I stood up, Dan grabbed my hand gently and said, "Okay, lovely." I smiled, though my eyes felt heavy with tiredness, and whispered goodnight before walking away quickly, not trusting myself to stay if I lingered. I was exhausted but also scared of getting into trouble. I really cared about Dan, and the last thing I wanted was for my dad to embarrass me in front of him. Besides, I knew we were going to his flat the next day, and, if I was honest, the thought made me a little nervous.

I must have fallen asleep fully dressed because, when I woke up in the morning, I was still in yesterday's clothes. I grabbed some fresh ones and had a shower before heading into the lounge to find Dan. I offered him a towel in case he fancied a shower too, but he smiled and said he'd wait until he got home since he didn't have any clean clothes with him. I teased him, saying, "You can borrow my knickers if you like," and we both laughed. He gave me a look and replied, "Very funny. I'll have to get cleaned up later though; I'm hoping I'll need to."

I hadn't really thought about him not having a shower beforehand. If I was honest, I was more nervous about being alone with him in his flat than anything else. I asked what time we were going, and he told me later. Then, almost as if sensing my disappointment, he added, "I might pop home for a bit and come back for you later. As long as I get you by five, we can still catch the top ten in the charts."

My heart sank a little. Even though the thought of going to his flat scared me, the idea of being without him felt worse. But I understood; he'd stayed over, probably had chores to do, and wanted to sort himself out before we spent time together.

He laughed then and said, "What an idiot; the charts aren't even on today. Shall we change it to tomorrow?" He grinned and gave me a playful poke. I'd already asked Mum if she minded me going, and she'd said of course not, which made me feel better about it.

When Dan finally came back, it felt like he hadn't even been gone, as I'd been busy watching Saturday TV shows with my parents and drinking endless cups of tea. I opened the door, and he suggested heading to his flat. I told him I'd let my parents know, and he said he'd come in to say hello. He greeted them, promised to look after me, and they laughed.

We left together, walking hand in hand. It was only a mile or so down the road, but it felt so grown-up. Even though we hadn't known each other long, it just felt right being together. Dan lived down a narrow, stony road in a council estate. On one side, there were houses surrounded by tall bushes with little gates and winding paths, though you couldn't see much of the houses through the greenery, apart from one where the gate hung broken from its hinges.

At the end of the road, we reached a larger house, split into two flats. Dan's was the one on the right, the first you came to, with a shingle driveway leading to the back door, the only one he had a key for.

When we arrived, no one else was home. We went straight to his room, where I flopped onto the bed while he pottered around, tidying up. In that moment, he seemed different somehow, more grown-up, and it made me feel slightly uneasy. It wasn't a bad feeling, just unfamiliar. I sat quietly, my mind racing with thoughts about what I was doing there, alone in a flat with a boy who felt much more like a man in this setting.

Dan must have sensed it because he gave me a hesitant smile as though trying to reassure me. He offered to make a cup of tea and, as he brushed past, kissed me on the cheek before disappearing. The door shut quietly behind him, leaving me alone with my thoughts, and not all of them were good.

I questioned myself: was I unsure because I was scared, or was it simply because it was all so new to me? I sat there quietly, taking in everything around the room. It was the neatness that unsettled me a little. I hadn't had much experience of that, and it felt strange, almost intimidating, to be with a man so different from me. He seemed so grown up, far beyond his years, while I was, in truth, still incredibly immature, and yet, he didn't seem to mind. But here, in this unfamiliar space, I found myself doubting him. The door began to open, jolting me from my thoughts. Dan stepped in and looked straight into my eyes as he passed me my drink. He even brought it in on a tray, which made me laugh in spite of myself. He smiled, and in that moment, the awkwardness I'd felt started to fade. He sat down on the bed beside me and, slowly, my heart began to race. I felt it skip a beat. After finishing our drinks, we lay down together. He began kissing me and my stomach flipped with nerves and excitement. I was wearing jeans, and soon he was undoing the buttons and gently unzipping them. My thoughts started to spiral, so I tried to steady myself by keeping busy. I reached for his T-shirt and started pulling it over his head. There wasn't much resistance from him; in fact, none at all. His T-shirt was white and thick, and he'd looked so good in it, though, I quickly realised, he looked even better without it.

He was very thin, his chest slightly concaved at the top, and I could see every rib along his torso. His stomach was completely flat, but I didn't mind; to me, he looked lovely. I felt a little apprehensive as I began to pull down the zip of his jeans. He lifted his hips to help me ease them off, and despite my nerves, excitement stirred within me at the thought of being so close to him like this, without barriers. He had already managed to undress me down to my bra and knickers, which I was still comfortable with, and he still had his pants on too. I noticed his penis hardening and, for reasons I couldn't explain, I felt a laugh bubble up. It sounded childish and silly to my ears, but Dan only laughed with me and gently pulled me closer.

"Are you on contraception?" he asked suddenly. The question caught me off guard.

"Oh no, I'm not," I admitted, feeling slightly embarrassed that I hadn't even thought about it.

"Don't worry, I've got condoms," he reassured me, and I watched as he calmly put one on with what felt like impressive ease. There was something about his

146

movements, so certain and unfazed, that made me quietly admire him.

We kissed and cuddled, and he held me softly before easing me onto my back. "Are you ready for me?" he asked. The question felt awkward in the middle of everything, and I was too shy to answer, so I pressed my tongue into his mouth to silence him. I was sure that if we started chatting, the moment would completely unravel.

As he began touching my nipples, they stiffened under his touch, as did his erection. His hand moved down my stomach, making me squirm when he reached my belly button, a sensation that made me giggle. That only seemed to encourage him. He started pressing himself near my opening, but it wasn't quite happening. I felt strangely responsible, not knowing what I should do. Dan tried to guide himself in with his fingers, without much success, and then, smiling, said, "Oh, I know." He started kissing and licking down my stomach, and I felt that bubbling giggle return. His tongue moved lower, sending shivers through me, and my body reacted naturally. My nipples tingled again, hardening, while the warmth built lower down as his mouth explored me.

When he finally moved back up, crawling over me, I could feel the heat radiating between us. He kissed me deeply, grabbing himself once more to guide him in, and this time he pressed hard into me. A groan escaped my lips, not from pleasure, but pain. It hurt, more than I had expected.

"Are you okay?" he asked, concern in his voice. I smiled quickly and kissed him again to avoid the conversation, unwilling to lose the moment or have it turn awkward. I didn't want to explain how that pain had always accompanied sex for me, nor how numb I was to it by now. I told myself it was normal, that it hurt for everyone at first.

It was a relief when it was over, and though the pain had been sharp when he first entered me, it faded quickly enough. Compared to my past experience with Ryan, this was almost tender. At least with Dan, I felt cared for, and that meant everything.

When it finished, he pulled me close and asked if I'd enjoyed it.

"Yes," I replied softly. "It was lovely." I didn't mention the pain.

Dan got up and made a cup of tea for us both, showing that same attentiveness he always did. He genuinely seemed to like looking after me, making sure I was comfortable and happy. We didn't talk about our future, neither of us had to. It just felt easy between us, like words weren't necessary. Back at home, though, things were different. My parents had begun pressuring me about my future. They wanted me working full-time, and since I'd left school with nothing, college wasn't an option. I was frightened about what lay ahead, and though being with Dan gave me moments of calm, that fear was always waiting for me when I went home.

Not long before, I had fallen out with my mum. My dad, clearly weary of the tension, said to me, "If you upset your mother again, you're no longer welcome in my house."

His words astounded me and, in truth, frightened me. It struck me, in that moment, just how close I was to having no home, to being entirely on my own. I felt uncertain about my future. I had spent years being criticised and told I was stupid, and, as a result, my self-esteem was fragile at best. I left school with very little in the way of qualifications or exam passes, and stepping out into the world to find a job felt like an enormous, almost impossible, challenge.

I had applied for a YTS job in Lymington, and as it happened, my brother's girlfriend had secured an opportunity there too. It was flexi-hours, which didn't suit me very well. I owed loads of hours and, truthfully, I didn't like the people there. They just had me sorting out endless piles of old filing that must have been sitting there for years; it was mind-numbingly boring. It wasn't that I was afraid of hard work, but the problem was nobody had time to teach me anything, and I felt completely overlooked.

Tracy, my brother's girlfriend, had a better position than me in the telephone department. I would have loved to work there too. Most days, we'd go into Lymington town centre together at lunchtime, and that was one of the few things I looked forward to. I used to get a lift into work with a local lady, paying her five pounds a week. She was kind, easy to talk to, and we'd chat about all sorts of things. But, if I'm honest, I didn't last long in that job. I found myself wishing I'd stayed on full-time at the garage instead. It made me feel thick and useless, and some days I honestly felt like crying before going in. To make matters worse, they told me they didn't think the job suited me and that I might be better off somewhere else. The only silver lining was that they agreed to pay me in full and wouldn't deduct the hours I owed. I was due to see Dan later, and I didn't want to tell him. I felt embarrassed, useless, and so low about it all. I even considered lying, saying I didn't like it and was applying somewhere else. What was wrong with me? I kept wondering.

When I saw Dan that evening, I told him I was going to apply for another job in Dibden, as I'd already been told they would place me there. It made me feel a little better. I already felt useless enough without having to confess to the man I'd grown to love how lost and inadequate I often felt. I didn't understand why I wasn't like other people, why I never seemed to fit in anywhere. I never felt truly confident in anything I did. The week passed quickly, and before I knew it, I was due to start the new job on Monday. By now, it had become routine for me to spend weekends at Dan's, although I wouldn't go round until Saturday afternoon because he liked to get his chores done in the morning. That Saturday, he came to collect me and asked if I was excited about starting work on Monday. He said it would be nice because we could have lunch together, as he worked in Dibden too.

When we got back to his place, we put some music on, as we often did, and it wasn't unusual for things to become intimate between us during those moments. I especially loved Lady in Red by Chris de Burgh, and somehow, it always seemed to be playing when we made love. I don't think it was ever planned; it was simply in the charts at the time and on the radio a lot. It was September now, and we'd already told each other that we were in love.

That afternoon, Dan took my hand, pulled me into a cuddle, and asked me to marry him. Without hesitation, I said yes. We kissed, and in that moment, I felt so happy, so safe, like everything was finally falling into place. I didn't have to be afraid of being homeless anymore, and for the first time, I had a future to hold onto. I looked at Dan and smiled, wondering how on earth I was going to tell my parents, though in that moment, it didn't seem to matter. All that mattered was us. I felt stronger with him, and the good thing was my parents liked him, so I told myself it would be fine. We spent the rest of the day together, making love, the pain easing a little more each time, although it was still there. But by then, I'd convinced myself it was normal. Later, as we lay cuddling, Dan gently said, "Come on, we'd better get you home." I was still glowing from the happiness of the engagement and feeling so wanted that I didn't mind leaving. As I started to get dressed, I reached for my knickers, and as I pulled them up, there was a sharp twang, and the elastic snapped. I felt myself blush as Dan, having both seen and heard it, burst into laughter.

"Can I borrow a pair of your pants to walk home in, please?" I asked, embarrassed.

He just kept laughing, saying, "Twang!" over and over. I couldn't help but find it funny too, though I wasn't keen on walking down the road without underwear. Dan said, "Just put your shorts on without them; no one will know." I wasn't sure about wearing his pants either, so I slipped into my shorts, knickerless, and felt a little bit cheeky. As we walked home, about halfway there, Dan suddenly shouted, "Twang!" and I couldn't stop laughing. It became like our little secret code, and we laughed almost the entire way home. It felt warm and safe being with him, like I finally belonged somewhere and, for once, someone truly cared about me.

When we were alone that evening, Dan asked, "Are you going to tell your parents?" I replied, "Not yet, no," thinking to myself that they would be furious. I told him I would speak to Mum first and had planned to do so nearer the following weekend, as that was when we were planning to go and get the rings. Dan seemed to have everything mapped out for us. We even talked about me moving in with him. He suggested we wait until October, as he was receiving housing benefit and that would need to be updated. I agreed without question, I trusted everything he said, taking it as gospel. I smiled, feeling a kind of happiness that was still quite new to me ever since I had met him.

The evening passed quickly, and Mum got the blanket down so Dan could stay on the sofa. He had started staying most weekends now, though always in the lounge, and that was fine by me. I usually went to bed when I felt tired, as I had an underlying fear of Dad walking into the lounge and finding me there with him. Dad knew we were sexually active, but sleeping in the same bed would not have been tolerated. It would have been seen as a sign of disrespect towards my parents.

Chapter 13: Facing the Mirror

My parents were a mixed bag, really. They could be very easy-going and kind about some things, yet when I truly needed them, they were next to useless. I used to be able to talk to my dad and find comfort in him, but as I grew older and started forming my own opinions, he became less agreeable. He would snap quickly, leaving me confused, so I often chose to keep out of his way, not wanting to irritate him. I loved him dearly and would have done anything to gain his approval, but no matter how hard I tried, it never seemed to be enough. With Dan, it was different. I never felt I had to earn his approval; it was always given freely. Unlike with my parents, I never felt like I was constantly falling short. To be honest, I didn't even think my mum liked me. I hadn't particularly liked her either. She was cold and often cruel, calling me thick and teasing me about the size of my bust. Whenever we had company, she would make me the centre of her jokes, belittling and mocking me to entertain others.

But none of that seemed to matter anymore. Everything felt better now. For the first time in my life, I felt like I belonged to someone. The next morning, we had our usual cup of tea, and Dan suggested we go to his flat. He had quickly picked up on my dad's temper, and since Dad was back from working nights, Dan preferred to be out of the house before he woke up. He never spoke badly about my parents, but he was good at making sure we left at the right times. Dan didn't have much of a family either. His parents had thrown him out, and after staying with his sister for a while, she had done the same. It was something we had in common. So off we went to his flat, before Dad was up.

On the way, Dan pulled me close, whispered "Twang," and grinned, "Have you got any knickers on today?"

I laughed. "Yes, big, thick ones that won't break," I teased.

He pretended to look disappointed, and I ran off ahead, with him chasing after me. It turned the walk to his flat into a bit of a game. We were always like that, playful and light-hearted, and it just seemed to come naturally to us.

As we got closer to his flat, he caught up, took my hand, and asked, "So, when are you telling your parents about the engagement?"

"Give me a chance," I smiled. "I'll tell my mum first, maybe towards next weekend."

Then, as if a switch had flicked, I suddenly remembered that I had to start the YTS in Dibden the next day, and a sick feeling crept into my stomach. I went quiet.

Dan, as always, noticed. He had a way of knowing when something wasn't quite right with me. "You okay?" he asked gently.

"I've got to start in Dibden tomorrow," I said.

"Good," he replied with a smile. "We can have lunch together."

Just like that, the sick feeling lifted a little, and I managed a small smile. It was strange how he always seemed to know what to say to settle me. We spent the afternoon as we often did, having sex to the top ten charts and then getting dressed to head back to mine. On the way, he cheekily asked again, "Got your knickers on today?" I just giggled and ignored him.

I felt a little odd that day. It was a Sunday, and Sundays had never been good days for me growing up. They reminded me of my grandad visits, which still haunted me. I didn't even fully understand why, I just always felt cold and uneasy inside on Sundays, even if the weather was warm. It was still September, and although it had cooled down a little, it was about twenty degrees, far from the crisp chill of autumn and winter. But this year, it didn't seem half as bad. With Dan around, I actually managed to distract myself from those old, intrusive thoughts. Whenever my mind started to wander, I would find a way to change the subject or talk about something else, and it worked.

When we got home, we found the house empty, which immediately made me feel better. Mum had left us both a note saying she and Dad had gone to visit my Aunty Alison and Uncle Rob in Winchester. I knew that meant they wouldn't be back early, and I couldn't have been more pleased.

Dan and I spent the rest of the evening watching television and cuddling, though it was Sunday, so he had to go home that night. In a way, I was relieved because I knew I was starting my new job in the morning, and there were a few nerves quietly sitting at the back of my mind. The fact that the other company hadn't wanted me only made me more anxious about this new job. What if I was still useless? What if Dan realised I wasn't good enough and didn't want me anymore My mind wouldn't stop racing, and it was making me tired. I turned to Dan and told him I was going to head up to bed. He seemed a little surprised, as it was usually me asking him to stay a bit longer. But tonight, I just wanted to be alone. I felt weighed down by my own insecurity and needed some headspace, a little quiet to calm my thoughts and drift off to sleep, hoping they'd leave me alone for a while.

I kissed Dan and walked him to the door, thinking I'd make a cup of tea and go to bed. Mum and Dad were still out, and I'd already laid out my clothes for the morning on the chest of drawers. I poured my tea and went back into my bedroom, though a heavy feeling settled over me. My back had begun to ache, though at the time I didn't connect it with the uneasy thoughts on my mind. When I woke the next morning, it was late, and I had to rush out the door to catch the bus. In my hurry, I'd forgotten the money I'd meant to take with me.

Despite that, I liked the idea of working in Dibden, especially knowing it was right by Dan's work. It made me feel a bit more excited about my first day. I'd always been good at pushing my fears aside. Growing up as I had, I'd developed coping mechanisms to handle my anxieties, and today was no different. When I arrived, the building didn't look much like a workplace at all. It resembled a wooden shack, with the entrance tucked around the back, and it was dark inside.

The first room I stepped into was empty. I half-expected someone to be there to greet me, but no one was. I carried on and soon spotted a woman typing away. She looked to be in her fifties, though there wasn't a trace of grey in her hair. Her face showed her age a little, but she was still quite pretty, and her fingers danced across the typewriter keys with astonishing speed. She didn't even look down at what she was doing. Watching her made me nervous. Would they be expecting the same from me? I could barely type, and I always had to look at the keys. I felt bloated and uncomfortable and really needed the toilet, but it felt too awkward to ask straight away. I coughed softly, hoping to catch the woman's attention. It didn't work. So, I wandered through to the next room, where a man sat working, just as absorbed as the woman had been.

Then, to my relief, the woman appeared behind me. "You must be Mandy? We've been expecting you," she said.

I smiled, feeling awkward. "Yes, that's right. What should I do?"

To my dismay, it was much the same as my last job. They simply sat me in front of a typewriter and said, "Well, we know you can type, how about you start there?"

I was at a loss. I had no idea what I was meant to be doing, and I felt terribly out of place. I fed some paper

157

into the typewriter, but I didn't know how to set it properly and it kept going wonky. I fiddled with it, moving the paper this way and that, typing random bits, hoping someone might eventually come and show me how to do it properly.

As my discomfort grew and my bladder felt on the verge of bursting, an older lady popped her head round the door and said, "Mandy, would you mind taking some petty cash and popping out to get some biscuits?"

I jumped at the chance. Anything to get out of there. I already felt as uncomfortable as I had on my first day at Lymington. I'd barely been there ten minutes, and yet I already had that sinking, heavy feeling that this wasn't going to work out either. I'd hoped someone might teach me something, but no, it seemed I was meant to somehow just know, which I clearly didn't. After figuring out where the petty cash was kept, I knew I had to find the toilet before doing anything else. I felt damp and wondered if I'd actually wet myself from holding it in too long, though that had never happened before. Still, the day already felt so disastrous that anything seemed possible.

I asked someone where the toilets were, half-worried it might be seen as a stupid question, but to my surprise, they showed me. It was ironic; finding the toilet was something I could have managed on my own. Yet here they were, guiding me there, when earlier they'd left me stranded in front of a typewriter with no clue what to do.

The toilet door made me chuckle; it had a picture of a lady actually sitting on a toilet for the ladies, and I dreaded to think what might be on the men's. I rushed into a cubicle, desperate to see what was happening in my knickers. I quickly pulled them down but had to sit on the toilet almost immediately, afraid I might wet myself if I waited even a second longer. Then I realised what the problem was: my period had started, and my knickers were covered in blood. I felt a wave of embarrassment. I thought about how I'd need to get some sanitary towels and felt relieved we were meant to be going to the shops for biscuits. But then it hit me: I didn't have any money of my own.

I cleaned myself up as best I could. The blood was still wet in my pants, but there wasn't much I could do. I rubbed some toilet paper over it a few times until it stopped leaving marks on the tissue. I managed to find a sanitary towel in the dispenser and placed it in my knickers. There was blood on my thigh too, so I wet some tissue at the sink and returned to the cubicle to wipe it away. It all felt horrible, this new, unfamiliar place. No one was particularly unkind, but they weren't especially helpful either. I didn't feel like I was going to fit in here. Yet what choice did I have? In that moment, I so wished I'd stayed at the garage.

I finished up in the toilet and realised I had probably been longer than I thought. I wondered if anyone had noticed, but luckily, having Dan working nearby was a real blessing. I could pop in to ask him for some money on my way to buy the biscuits. I'd never visited his workplace without him expecting me, and I wasn't sure how it would be received. When I arrived at the garage, three men stood around and looked at me as if to ask what I wanted. I asked, "Is Dan here, please?" One of them replied, "Who's asking?" before saying he'd fetch him. A moment later, Dan appeared, having clearly come quickly from spraying a car, a concerned look on his face. "Are you alright?" he asked.

I explained, "I've no money, and I've had my monthly surprise with nothing to change with." He laughed, which, although not what I'd expected, probably helped because it made me feel a little lighter. I could feel the other men watching us, which made me self-conscious. Dan gave me a pound and said, I'll see you at lunch," before blowing me a kiss, much to his colleagues' amusement. I cringed a little as I left, feeling the weight of their stares on my back.

I headed to the shops and picked up some sanitary towels, suddenly remembering the biscuits. I wasn't sure what kind to buy, so I grabbed some chocolate ones and a pack of plain digestives too, always a safe option. I hurried back, worried I'd been gone too long and that they might think I'd vanished.

When I walked in, the older lady joked, "We thought you'd stolen the petty cash and gone home!" I cringed and apologised, explaining I'd had 'girl problems'. Her expression softened immediately. "Oh, I was only teasing," she said kindly. "What biscuits did you get?"

I told her, and she suggested, "Go and make the tea, and we'll have a break, what do you think?" I was relieved. At least I knew I could make a good cup of tea. Maybe I could impress them with that, and the biscuits seemed to be a hit.

In the kitchen, I started hunting for the cups, opening nearly every cupboard. Strangely, none of them seemed to hold any cups. I even tugged on cupboards that wouldn't open. How could something so simple be so

160

difficult? Feeling foolish, I gave up and went back to the lady's room. "I can't find the cups," I admitted.

She laughed. "Oh, sorry, that's our fault. We keep them in here because the night school lot never brings them back."

I felt relieved they didn't think I was stupid. She handed me the cups, and I returned to the kitchen. Lorna, which struck me oddly, as it was the same name as a friend of mine, noticed I hadn't taken a cup for myself. "You haven't got one for you," she said. I hadn't forgotten; I was simply too shy to help myself. I was grateful when she gave me a cup. I made all the teas, brought out the biscuits, and Lorna poured them into a tin with tiny butterflies on it. She set it on the table, open, and invited everyone to help themselves. There was no chance I would; I was far too shy. I hadn't had breakfast either and was hungrier than usual, probably because of my period. Watching them all tuck into the biscuits was torture.

"I'll just go back to the typing in my tray, if that's alright," I muttered.

"Of course, but finish your tea first," they replied. "You can take it with you if you like." I was glad for that. Janice, the younger one, gave me a kind smile as I left. There was a man there too, John, who looked oddly familiar, though I couldn't place where I knew him from. Perhaps he'd been a teacher at my school, not one who taught me directly, but someone I'd seen around. Being from the area, it could have been anywhere really.

I started typing and began to feel a little more comfortable. I'd been given a small task, which somehow felt homely, like I belonged, or at least like I was meant to be there. I had a feeling they might have forgotten I was due in earlier because everyone was making much more effort now than when I first arrived. I glanced at the clock and realised it was nearly lunchtime, which suited me perfectly because I was starving. I didn't have any money with me, but I'd already decided I would pinch Dan's lunch. I felt comfortable enough to do that now. He always brought loads because, being six foot four, he was constantly hungry.

I made my way to the wall where he'd said he would meet me and sat down, relieved to be out of the building for a while. I heard him coming up behind me, and he called out, "Hello, you." I smiled; it felt so nice just being near him after a morning of feeling overwhelmed in a place full of strangers and unfamiliar routines. He leaned in to kiss me and, with a grin, said, "As if by magic, here. I made you sandwiches because I knew you wouldn't have any, and you'd only pinch mine."

I laughed, wondering how he always seemed to know what I was thinking. Although he was right, I'd definitely planned to eat his.

He asked, "How's your period, were the towels okay?"

I told him it had gone through onto my knickers, but I'd put the towel over the blood and it was all dry now. I admitted how scared I'd been of being caught in the toilets because I'd had to clean the tops of my legs. I was so relieved no one had walked in while I was holding a wet tissue and heading back into the cubicle. I would have died, how could I have explained that?

He looked at me, trying not to laugh at the thought, but then his expression changed as he noticed my discomfort. Leaning over, he said kindly, "You poor thing, bad timing. But how are things going otherwise?"

I didn't want to tell him the truth, which was that I felt useless. Instead, I nodded and said, "So far, all good," forcing a smile to hide how I really felt. It was a habit I'd picked up from a difficult childhood, smiling to mask the fact you were breaking inside, never letting the world see your secret. The secret that made you feel like a terrible person, one who had somehow deserved the awful things your grandad had done. I quickly changed the subject in my mind, not wanting to linger there. I looked over at Dan and thought about how I'd ended up here, sitting on a wall, with a man who loved me. He'd made my lunch without being asked, and he wanted to marry me. How had this happened? In that moment, I felt more wanted than I ever had in my life. I belonged. Me. I actually belonged, well, at least with Dan, I did.

But as for work, I still didn't feel I belonged. The thought crossed my mind again as I asked him the time, realising I only had half an hour break. The trouble with being with Dan was that time seemed to vanish; like a Pac-Man gobbling up fruit, it disappeared before I knew it. I realised I'd have to get back; I had only three minutes of lunch left. I felt worse walking back to work. Being with

Dan had made me feel good after such a difficult morning, and now I knew I'd have to sit with that drained, awkward feeling all over again.

The people at work were kind enough, but I didn't feel like I fitted in. We hurried back, and Dan gave me a quick peck on the cheek before dashing back to his workshop. Normally I might have complained about such a brief goodbye, but there wasn't time for a proper kiss anyway. It was lovely having him nearby during the day; I just wished I'd felt more settled at work. I had a gut feeling things would go the same way they had in Lymington, but even faster this time.

Back in the office, I returned to the items in my tray, though I wasn't entirely sure what I was supposed to be doing. I didn't ask for clarification either, which, in hindsight, would have been sensible. But this was me, the girl who'd pooed her pants at primary school, so not much had changed in that respect. The afternoon passed more quickly than the morning, which was a relief, and before long they were sending me home. I didn't see Dan after work as he finished later than I did. I only worked until quarter past three, then had to catch the bus. Although, for my first day, Mum had kindly offered to collect me, though she'd reminded me it wasn't something she planned to do again. I'd expected as much. Why would I have thought otherwise?

I didn't mind the bus anyway. It gave me some time to myself.

Today, though, I just wanted to leave that office as fast as possible. It felt dark and miserable inside. The people

I worked with were nice enough but much older than me and a little hippyish. I wasn't used to being around so many older people, and there was no one else my age there. I hurried past Dan's workplace, wondering if he'd see me, though he was probably inside spraying a car. As I turned the corner, I spotted Mum waiting in her car, and it felt unexpectedly nice seeing her there. For a moment, I wanted to run up and throw my arms around her because I felt so lonely.

As I reached for the car door, she asked, "So how did it go?"

At that, my heart sank.

"I'm not sure," I admitted.

She offered the usual reassurance, "It's only your first day. You're bound to feel like that, it's all new."

But deep down, I knew I wasn't imagining it. Things weren't going to get any better. Still, I went along with her enthusiasm for now. I was hungry again; every time I had my period, I felt constantly hungry, and today was no different. I asked what we were having for dinner, and when she said curry, I was thrilled. It was one of my favourites. On the way home, I asked if I could borrow some money, half-expecting a refusal. But she must have been in a good mood because she asked what I wanted it for. I told her, and when we stopped at the shop for her bits, I stayed in the car. When she came back out, she handed me some chocolates and crisps. I smiled up at her, and after the day I'd had, it felt really good.

A feeling of relief washed over me, and I knew my evening would be far better than my day had been. Although I was already dreading work tomorrow, I'd managed to push it to the back of my mind, my usual way of coping. I knew Dan would be round later, and the thought of having a proper cuddle made me feel a bit better. Truthfully, I felt like I needed one now. A part of me still wished I'd stayed on at the garage. I'd felt good at my job there, and at least they took the time to teach me what to do. They hadn't just thrown me in at the deep end and expected me to figure everything out on my own. Even at school, they would explain things first. It left me a bit confused now. Was I missing something? Did they assume I already had experience? Surely having a Pitman qualification in typing wouldn't have led them to believe I could just walk into an office and be a secretary without any guidance.

I didn't understand it. How was I supposed to know what to do in a job I'd never been shown? Yet, because of my low self-esteem, I automatically blamed myself. I felt like there was something wrong with me, that I was somehow at fault for not being able to read their minds. My Pitman course had been nothing more than a typing exam, knowing how to load paper into a typewriter and type, basically. But these people seemed to expect me to arrive and instantly know the job inside out. And here I was, feeling inadequate because they hadn't bothered to train me.

I went into my bedroom, put my things away and changed out of my work clothes. As I headed towards the kitchen to make myself a cup of tea, I paused. I could hear voices, one of them a man's and I immediately wondered who was in the house. As I stepped into the kitchen, I saw Ryan standing there. He looked straight at me and said, "Hi, how are you?"

It felt strange. Even though I really liked Dan, my heart sank a little at the sight of Ryan. I realised in that moment I still missed him, still fancied him, though I kept those feelings firmly hidden. I looked down, not wanting him to catch any trace of what might still be in my eyes. "I'm great, thanks. I'm going out with Dan now," I said, as casually as I could.

"I've heard... but you're mine," he replied.

I looked up again, trying to work out if he was joking. I studied his face, watching his body language for any clue as to what he actually meant. I wondered where my brother was; surely Ryan hadn't come round to see my parents? As it turned out, he'd come with his brother, who'd been sorting out some electrical work for my mum and dad. I grabbed my tea as quickly as I could and headed back to my bedroom, but I could sense Ryan following behind me. His presence was beginning to make me feel uneasy. Why was he following me?

"How are you?" he asked again, like he hadn't believed my answer in the kitchen.

"Like I said, I'm fine. I'm happy," I replied, though my voice was sharper this time. "I'm not too keen on my new job, but I haven't told Mum yet, so don't say anything."

"That's a shame. Why don't you like it?" he asked.

167

"I just don't know what's expected of me. No one's explained anything properly; they just stuck me in a room and expected me to start typing."

"Well, you should ask them if you're unsure. I'm sure they'd tell you."

His comment irritated me. "I did ask," I snapped, "and they still didn't explain." He wasn't making me feel better about any of it, in fact, he was making me feel worse. I sighed, feeling frustrated. "Anyway, why did you even come round with Aidan?"

"To see you of course."

I was a bit annoyed. All the years I hadn't had boyfriends, he'd hardly spoken to me. He would come round with whatever girl he fancied at the time, acting like it pleased him. Now, suddenly, with a bit of competition, he was trying to mark his territory and change his tune. I shrugged and said, "Well, Dan will be here later, so I need to get a shower and get ready."

He looked at me in that knowing way, and I could feel how smug he was. It was as though he knew I still loved him, like he could see that part of me that wanted his mouth on mine, even now. Yet here he was, making me suffer the loss of him all over again. The real reason his behaviour bothered me so much was because it brought questions to the surface and made me doubt whether I really loved Dan. With that thought weighing on me, I knew I needed to push Ryan away. I blurted out, "Well, I'm marrying Dan."

He laughed like it was some sort of joke. "You've only just met him," he said.

It Is Not How Life Starts, It Is How You Finish It

My stomach churned. I instantly regretted saying it. No one else knew yet, and the thought of Ryan going and telling my parents filled me with anxiety. If they found out like that, there would be hell to pay. I wanted my mum to know first, before Dad. I needed her approval so I could be sure before facing him. If I could convince her it was a good idea, maybe she would help talk Dad round. That was always how things worked in our house.

Trying to deflect, I said, "Is Aidan wanting you? I think I heard someone call." I desperately wanted to be left alone. I could feel tears threatening and wondered when the pain of losing him was ever going to leave me alone. When I was with Dan, I felt happy and safe; it didn't feel wrong. But when Ryan was around, all the old feelings came flooding back.

The fact that, for once, I actually wanted him to go made me feel a little better. Normally, I'd find any excuse to keep him there longer. But here I was, trying to get rid of him. I just wanted a bit of time to myself. Dan would be round later, and I needed space to clear my head.

Thankfully, Ryan left the room. I heard voices by the door; it must have been Aidan calling him, and then Dad closed the door behind them. A minute later, my bedroom door opened and Dad popped his head in.

"Are you okay?" he asked.

I looked up at him. "Yes, I'm good," I replied.

"Dinner will be ready soon," he told me, and I nodded.

"Mum said you had a good day at work."

I nodded again, feeling like a complete fraud. I gave him an awkward smile, but inside I wanted to cry. I hated lying to my dad. I was usually honest with him about everything, and keeping this inside made me feel low. I was properly on the edge of tears now. I stayed in my room for about an hour, until I heard Dad calling me down for dinner.

I jumped up straight away because I was starving. I still had my chocolates and crisps waiting for me, but dinner had to come first. I was looking forward to those treats afterwards though. As I pulled my chair out at the table, Mum passed me my curry. It wasn't often we all sat down and ate together these days.

"Mandy's got some treats to share after dinner," Mum said.

My heart sank again. Mum never bought treats just for me, and today I'd let myself believe those goodies were mine. Now I realised they were for sharing. And in our house, sharing meant I probably wouldn't get much of anything. It was always a bit of a free-for-all when there was chocolate, biscuits, or crisps, like a pack of wolves, and then it was all gone. Oh well, I thought, maybe Dan would walk to the shop with me tonight, and we could pick out some decent stuff. I had loads of money in my drawer, and I still owed him some anyway.

It Is Not How Life Starts, It Is How You
Finish It

The dinner was delicious. I asked if there was any more, and Mum said yes, which made me really happy. I was always extra hungry when I was due on my period. I should've known it was coming because the night before, my back had ached; it always did the night before. I didn't often get stomach cramps, but the back pain was enough. I thought to myself, what us girls have to go through. Still, at least now Dan might start making me lunch sometimes; I could definitely get used to that. It felt nice being looked after for once. Mum had never been that bothered about breakfast. She was always at work when I went to school, either already gone or about to leave, so I suppose she'd just assumed it was there if I wanted it. Though half the time, I'd make myself a sugar sandwich.

In an attempt not to feel left out or unloved, I said I'd bring the sweets in but added that I was too full and wouldn't be having any myself. It felt a bit like I was cutting off my nose to spite my face, but the way I saw it, if I made a point of not having any, then I wouldn't be bothered when they were all taken before I'd even had a chance. I went back into my room and, truthfully, I was quite full. I'd never been that keen on sweet stuff anyway; it always left me feeling a bit sick and guilty afterwards. Besides, I had enough money now that if I really wanted any, I could buy my own. But, in all honesty, I didn't much care. Before long, the door went and it was Dan. He asked if I was alright and I gave a half-hearted shrug. "I feel rubbish because of my period," I admitted, "but apart from that, I'm good." I pulled him into a big hug, grateful for the comfort.

Chapter 14: Choosing Peace

We lay down and just relaxed that evening, and the next day we met for lunch. We decided we'd do that daily. I was starting to settle in a little at work now, even feeling confident enough to chat with them, laugh, and share a joke. I still didn't feel I truly knew what I was doing though. They all seemed to get on with their own work, and it still felt a little awkward at times. This carried on for about a month, until one afternoon I got a call from the YTS lead. The moment I answered, I could tell something was wrong. They said the people at Dibden didn't feel it was working out. I held my breath. I felt my throat tighten, my fist clenching in an effort to contain the pain rising inside me. I pressed my tongue against my teeth to distract myself, but it didn't help.

It wasn't just the words; it was what they confirmed. The deepest fear I carried, planted by my mother's voice over the years, was now real: I was thick, as she'd always called me. Useless. I felt that old familiar wave of helplessness crash over me, drowning me in loneliness once more. From that moment on, I barely heard another word. My mind had already spiralled into a dark corner, revisiting all those feelings of worthlessness and the dread of having to tell my mother. I knew what was coming, the ridicule, the look of confirmation on her face that she'd been right all along. The thought of it made my hands clammy and my eyes sting. The conversation on the phone had already ended, though I hadn't heard the last of it. Another failing. I knew I'd be asked how the call was left, and I wouldn't know. Why didn't I ask? Why am I always so scared?

I hesitated to put the receiver down, as if delaying the inevitable might somehow save me. But of course, it couldn't. With a deep breath, I placed it back and hurried to my room. For a moment, I felt a surge of relief; Mum hadn't asked about the call. I'd gotten away with it. At least for now. But tomorrow, when I didn't go to work, she'd know. And the fear of that made my stomach churn. I lay on my bed, trapped inside my own head. The thought of being so useless ate away at me, and I started to worry about Dan. Would he still want me once he realised what I was? Would he see how stupid I was? Would he leave too? I was almost glad he wasn't coming round that evening; it was his night out with the lads, and for once, I needed to be alone.

I went into the kitchen to make a cup of tea, grateful to find it empty. It gave me a moment's peace. But I knew I had to speak to Mum before morning. I had the number for the YTS admin team; I could ring them in the morning and hope they'd place me somewhere else. Though, with two failed placements already, my confidence was crumbling. Maybe Mum was right. Maybe I really was dumb. While not looking forward to my mum confirming it yet again. Having more ammunition to tell everyone who came round how stupid I was. I took my tea, and as I was about to leave, Mum walked in. She asked, "Are you still enjoying your new job?" My heart started pounding. Did she know? It was the first time she'd asked since my first day. I froze. I could hardly breathe, and before I could think, I blurted it out. "They called… they said I'm not getting on." I blurted it out and wanted to get the ridiculing over with as soon as possible. Although that wasn't mum's style, she didn't really ridicule me while we were alone it wasn't half as much fun for her without company to witness it.

The room was still and quiet and she said, "Oh, no surprise there then. Why aren't you trying?" It stung, but I didn't answer. What was the point? She wouldn't hear the truth. That no one really told me what to do, that I felt awkward and unwelcome. She wasn't interested in facts. Only in reaffirming my failings.

She didn't say another word. Just looked at me, turned, and left. No hug, no reassurance, no kind word. Just silence. That hurt more than the words would have. I stood in the kitchen with my tea, scared of what the future held. I didn't know what to do next. I wasn't sure if Dan would stay when he realised how useless I was. I felt utterly alone, isolated and cold inside.

I was dreading the next day, the thought of having to speak to the YTS team and once again feeling like a failure. But that was tomorrow's worry, not tonight's. I had a cup of tea in my hand and it tasted warm and comforting. There was something about the warmth of tea; it felt like a hug in a mug. Perhaps that's why I always had one on the go, twenty-four-seven. It was my cuddle in the morning, my comfort in the evening, and my companion throughout the day. It made up for the affection I'd never really been given, the kind of action that says "I love you" without having to

175

speak the words. My parents were good at saying those words; they told me all the time that they loved me. But there was never any real action to back it up, no tenderness or warmth that made those words mean anything.

I spent a lot of time at my Auntie's house, and she'd mentioned more than once how cold those words sounded coming from my parents. "They say it a lot," she told me. "But, where's the affection?" At the time, I didn't quite understand what she meant. Her own past had left her unable to say those words easily, though she was better at showing love through her actions, especially to my cousin. But even then, there were mixed messages. It wasn't much better, really. Laura suffered in her own way because Pat was pretty damaged herself. Although she loved Laura, I don't think she ever quite managed to show it properly either. And Laura had her own struggles, living in a home where her father would beat her mother. It wasn't much better than the situation I'd grown up in, just another type of dysfunctional family, one more chapter in a long line of historical pain and cycles of abuse being repeated without anyone fully realising it was happening.

I sipped my tea, the warmth seeping into my hands, and closed my eyes, letting my imagination sweep me away from reality. In my fantasy world, I was cherished, loved, and safe. Since meeting Dan, the need for rescue had faded; he'd already saved me in ways I hadn't dreamed possible. I leaned back, picturing our future: the wedding we'd plan, the life we'd build. The vision was so vivid that when I opened my eyes, it was morning.

I slipped out of bed and padded to the kitchen for my morning ritual, a cup of tea, my liquid hug. Its heat radiated through me, a comforting substitute for the maternal warmth I'd never known. Tea had become my anchor, a way to drown the despair that lingered in my bones. Alone in the quiet house, I knew I had to make the call, but first, I'd savour this moment. Maybe I'd shower, too. My thoughts drifted to what I'd wear, had Mum washed my favourite jumper? I'd tossed it in the laundry yesterday, and she was usually quick to return it, clean and folded.

Mum wasn't the warmest parent, but she met my needs with precision. Dinner was always on the table, and my clothes were always ironed, unless I'd lazily dumped them on my bedroom floor. Not always the clothes I wanted, mind you. Sensible, expensive ones, chosen for me. We weren't poor, far from it. Dad called himself working-class, but with one of the best-paying jobs in the area and the guest house they ran, money was never an issue. Middle-class or not, we were comfortable. Yet it bothered me to some degree having all the best clothes in photos. It was always made to look like such a proper family with money and all well-kept. Yet I saw this as a facade because I was being sexually abused by Grandad and my dad was beating my mum up in front of me and rowing most of the time. It felt fake, all the pictures looking like the perfect family yet. A visual display of a wholesome, well-kept family, yet here was I, the unhappiest child in the world. Being punished for being thick and sexually abused from an age I was not sure of; it had always been the way it had been from my earliest memory. Along with that, I watched my lovely daddy beat my mummy up and yet the picture told a lie and I hated it. It felt like a mockery!

I found my jumper and felt an instant lift in my spirits. My sister had bought it for me, and its loose fit hid my figure, exactly what I needed. I'd always loathed my body; it felt like a betrayal, as if it advertised a sexuality I never chose. Tight clothing invited leers and lewd comments from men, and, worse still, the snug fabric would trigger memories of abuse. It was as though Grandad's hands were pressing against me again. So I lived in baggy clothes, keeping those memories firmly locked away.

In my mind, those memories lived behind a heavy door secured with a huge key. Tight clothes were sometimes that key, and when they forced the door open, I'd be flooded with fear, sadness and helplessness. To cope, I'd eat or smoke, anything to distract myself from the pain. But each distraction was only temporary. The life I'd left behind, the world of sex, lies and silence, still haunted me. Dan wanted to marry me, and in him I saw my exit from that mess, from the false reality I'd endured.

Even my dad used to disgust me. He would grope my mum's breasts as if she existed solely for his pleasure. He'd remark about women on the television, "She's got a nice pair of boobs, wouldn't mind going to bed with her." Hearing him talk like that made me physically sick. It was not the image I wanted for my own life. I did not want a man who ogled other women or treated his partner as an object.

Dad's behaviour made me question everything. If Grandad, my own grandfather, could violate me despite being married to Nan, why should I trust any man? Dad's crude remarks only deepened my confusion and disgust. I resented him and made no secret of it. He would snap back, "There's nothing wrong with it, there's something wrong with you." But I knew in my heart that no man would ever treat me the way he treated Mum. I vowed I would leave any man who did.

My mind became a tangle of contradictions: I loved Dad, yet hated him in the same breath. When his words or actions turned cruel, I'd walk away and retreat into my imagination, conjuring kinder, safer places. Sometimes I'd go for long walks, losing myself in the wind, the rustle of leaves and the hum of passing cars. Being outdoors helped me shut that locked room of memories and focus on something positive instead. I became good at packing away the bad and holding onto whatever good I could find.

Now it was time to make the call. With all these thoughts running through my mind, I found the idea of speaking to someone almost easier, a welcome distraction from everything else. I asked to speak to the man who had been assigned to me but was told he wasn't available. Instead, a lady offered to help. Oddly, this felt like a relief. I didn't know her, so it seemed easier somehow. What did it matter what she thought of me? I felt free to say exactly what had happened, how I'd been left not knowing what to do, how it had made me feel, how nothing had been explained. And to my surprise, she agreed with me. "It's not your fault," she said.

Those words. I wasn't prepared for the effect they'd have. It felt so good to hear them; I wanted to hear them again and again. So I repeated what had happened, and she calmly listened before saying, "I understand, let me call you back."

For a moment, the phone went quiet and I feared she'd hung up on me. But then I heard her voice again, reassuring and steady. "I'll sort this out and find you another placement."

It was like music to my ears. The call I had dreaded had somehow left me feeling lighter. As I placed the receiver down, I realised my lips were curling into a smile. Her words echoed in my head: It's not your fault. Words I had longed to hear, not just for this, but for so many things in my life.

These were words I wasn't really used to hearing. It felt strangely comforting, her saying them to me, and I liked it more than I probably should have. Afterwards, I went to have a shower, only to realise I'd forgotten to take any towels in with me. By the time I noticed, I was soaked, and there wasn't even a small hand towel I could use to dry off a bit before getting out. The floor would be slippery now, and for a moment I worried I might fall. Though I was alone in the house, being from a big family meant you could never be entirely sure no one was about to walk in. Dad worked shifts, and I never quite knew where he might be, and the last thing I wanted was for him to catch sight of me like that. But I had no choice. I had to get a towel from the airing cupboard in the hallway, right in full view of the front door. Here goes, I thought, rushing out into the hallway, leaving puddles behind me and feeling my flesh wobble as

I moved. I hated that feeling, so I tried to ignore it. I flung open the cupboard and grabbed the nearest towel, not caring whether it was mine. I just wanted to get dry and dressed as quickly as possible.

Luckily, I managed it with no one walking in, and afterwards I felt oddly content, sitting about waiting for the call. For the first time, I realised I'd let go of that awful fear of disapproval, that constant dread of not knowing what to do. But then it struck me: Dan still didn't know I'd lost my job, and he'd probably turn up at lunchtime expecting to see me. I glanced at the clock. It was half past eleven, and we were meant to meet at twelve. The calm I'd held on to from earlier was quickly starting to slip away. What will I do? I thought. Well, the truth was there wasn't much I could do. I was sure Dan would understand, and yet a horrible thought crept in: what if he didn't? What if he started to think I was useless? What if he didn't want me anymore?

I was so pleased to have a boyfriend. It felt good, new and fresh, and, for once, my brother couldn't interfere because he didn't really know him. They were in the same school year, though I don't think they properly knew each other, just friends of friends. Then a wave of sadness came over me. I'd been hopeless at my job. I really had wanted to learn, but it never quite happened. I was always too afraid to ask questions, though I could never fully explain why. It was as though I carried around this sense of not being wanted, of being a nuisance, and even my mum didn't help. She'd called me thick for as long as I could remember, and somewhere along the way, I'd believed them. At school, I'd lived up to it, too. I barely did any work after a while. I gave up because no one really helped me, and I didn't want to cause a fuss or draw attention to myself. I hated the idea of people looking at me, fearing what might happen if they did.

That fear, though imagined most of the time, had come from years of home life where Mum shouted at me for the smallest things, Dad shouted at Mum or at us kids, and my siblings picked on me endlessly. It was awful, and it made me scared to speak up, especially about anything to do with learning. I grew up believing I was stupid and, worse, I acted like it too. So much of it was down to fear. I didn't ask because I assumed I couldn't do anything, even though I'd never really tried. I was stuck in a vicious cycle, and I knew it.

Anyway, my thoughts were distracted when I heard the phone ring. I snapped out of my head and lunged for the receiver, picking it up quickly. I stayed quiet for a second until I heard the lady ask for me, and I replied, "Yes, it's Mandy." I waited, holding my breath, wondering what she was going to say and whether I'd feel comfortable with what she was about to tell me. It was times like this I really wished I'd stayed at the garage full-time. It didn't even cross my mind that I could ask Daniel if I could go back there. It was like my brain had been trained not to ask questions, just to do as I was told. That way there was less chance of getting into trouble, less chance of being shouted at.

The lady told me I was going to be working in Owen and Owen, the department store my mum used to shop at in Southampton. She went on to explain that I'd need a uniform and started telling me my working hours. Straight away my mind started racing. How was I going to get to Southampton on the bus? My head went ten to the dozen, and I felt sick with worry all over again. I really wished at that moment that I'd asked a few more questions about the typing job in Dibden. Because now I was facing getting a uniform and travelling two hours a day just to get there and back, and it felt like too much. I knew Mum would make me do it anyway. There was no chance I'd be allowed to turn it down.

Dan and I had planned to move in together in October, and since it was already September, it wasn't far off. Still, I knew my parents would continue to hold some influence over me, though I assured myself it wouldn't be quite so much. Dan and I had even spoken about having a child together. We both agreed it would be better to wait until we were living in our own place, though, in truth, I was eager to have a baby. In my mind, having a child seemed like a solution. I imagined it would relieve me of the pressure to keep a job, as I would have someone to care for instead. I hadn't really considered how I would balance a baby with work, the practicalities never crossed my mind. All I thought about was how having a child would make me feel whole, give me someone to love without condition, and provide a way out of the life I was desperate to leave behind. It was, I suppose, a naive, teenage fantasy, but to me, it meant much more than that.

While I was lost in these thoughts, I realised the woman on the other end of the phone was still speaking, giving instructions about where I needed to go, what time to start and finish, and stressing that lateness would not be tolerated. She also reminded me about the uniform. It dawned on me, rather too late, that I hadn't written any of it down. Mustering my most polite voice, I asked if she minded if I got a pen. There was a brief silence before she said 'yes', as though it had already been assumed I was writing everything down as she spoke. Yet this didn't trouble me too much; people being irritated with me was so common I would have felt more uneasy had she not shown some annoyance.

To my surprise, I managed to find a pen fairly quickly. That was rare in our house, as people were always calling out for one. I remembered how Mum would often yell for a pen at the top of her voice, and it was usually me who rushed to fetch it, desperate to stop her shouting. This time, however, I struggled to find a clean piece of paper. In my panic, I grabbed a scrap from the table, noticing too late that something was already written on it. Afraid to keep the woman waiting any longer, I quickly turned it over and hoped it wasn't anything important. I worried that Mum might be furious later if she saw I had written on it.

When the call finally ended and the receiver went down, I felt utterly drained. My mind immediately turned to the job ahead, and I began dreading how those days would feel. The bus journey from where I lived to Southampton would take an hour, and I would then need to walk a further fifteen to twenty minutes to reach the place. For the first time, I realised how fortunate I had been working in Dibden, so close to home. At least I knew Mum would pay for the uniform. She was good like that. In truth, I had little to worry about financially. My parents could afford regular holidays; we went to France every year, and they often went away without us, leaving us with babysitters. We actually loved it when they went away. Dad's friends would look after us, keeping us entertained, making us laugh, and playing games. They spent more time with us than Mum and Dad ever did. Even Monopoly would come out, though the board rarely lasted more than a week or two.

Now the house was silent, and for a while, my thoughts settled. I noticed how dark the walls looked, standing alone in the hallway where the phone sat on a small table. Mum kept a doily and a frilled white tablecloth on it. There was a potted plant too, an ivy, I thought, trailing down towards the floor. I hadn't really noticed it before, and it looked more yellow than green, probably in need of water. I was tempted to water it for Mum, though I wasn't sure she'd appreciate it, so I decided it was safer to leave it alone and perhaps remind her later. It wasn't the sort of plant I'd choose for my home, not that I had one of my own yet. This made me realise something: I never really pictured the house I wanted to live in. I only ever imagined the man I'd be with.

I started looking around and it felt strange; the hallway seemed slightly dark, with the front door ahead of me and the space turning into an L-shape that grew gloomier as it led towards the lounge. I had this sudden, odd urge to notice the décor. It struck me as strange because we'd lived here for years and I'd never really paid much attention to it before. Though I did know there was wallpaper in the lounge with white and blue flowers on it, which actually looked quite posh. That hadn't been there

185

too long; I remembered because Mum and Dad had argued the whole time it was being put up, Dad shouting at Mum for cutting it wrong or something like that. I hated being around when they did DIY. It was always a guaranteed row, and I would instinctively look for an escape route, knowing Dad would inevitably win, whether through sheer aggression or outright violence. I'd learned to block most of their fights out because I couldn't bear the noise or the shouting, and deep down I knew it would end with Dad hitting Mum. That felt strange, because even though I never really felt close to her, I didn't like seeing her hurt.

I did love her. I just didn't like her sometimes, the way she made me feel so small and as though she despised me. She'd call me thick, tease me that I looked like a boy, and make jokes at my expense when people came round. I was her clown, the one she could mock to lift herself up, to feel superior. And yet, despite everything, I loved her and desperately wished she'd just love me back. It hardly ever happened. Mostly, what I got from her was shouting. I don't think she ever really knew how to be a mother. Maybe she was just tired and bitter about life. She'd told me more than once that she'd never wanted children, that she'd only had us because Dad wanted a family.

This didn't make me feel very loved, and I suppose the feelings of resentment stemmed from this kind of behaviour. While I was in the lounge, I noticed all the crystal ornaments Mum kept in a cupboard. I had never really paid much attention to material things around me before, but now, for some reason, I found myself interested, wanting to look at everything properly. I glanced at the fireplace and the carpet, which I had never liked because it was beige.

Who chooses a beige carpet, anyway? I smiled at the thought. It wasn't as though I usually cared about things like that, but I was certain I wouldn't have picked beige.

Just then, I heard someone come through the front door. It could have been anyone, although I secretly hoped it was Dad. His shifts were always unpredictable, and I never quite knew when he might be home. My brother should still have been at work, and Mum was definitely out. I went to the hallway to check, and there was my brother, stuffing a doughnut into his mouth.

"Hello, smelly. What you doing here?" he asked.

"I don't have a job at the moment," I replied.

"Skiver," he teased, pulling a face.

"Let me have a doughnut," I begged.

"Get lost," he said, disappearing into the kitchen.

I didn't bother following him. He'd only get annoyed, and besides, I didn't want to see him eating all the doughnuts when it was clear I wasn't getting one.

I went into my bedroom, wanting to feel alone by choice rather than because people didn't want me around. Somehow, it always felt better making that decision for myself. But today was turning out to be different. My brother called me.

"Mandy Pandy, do you want to play on my computer? I'm playing Nottingham Forest. You have to go through marshes, kill skeletons, get through each gate, and reach another level."

I couldn't believe he was asking me to play. "Yeah, okay!" I shouted back quickly and made my way into his room. I loved my brother so much. He meant a lot to me. It was strange; we weren't particularly close in a conventional sense, but there was an unspoken love between us. We all understood, without really saying it, what we'd been through as children and what, in many ways, we were still going through. It was a silent understanding, sometimes acknowledged and sometimes left unsaid, depending on how each day turned out.

I sat on his bed as he handed me a controller and showed me how to play. It didn't take long for me to get the hang of it. Oddly, he left the room while I was still playing. Time flew by, and every so often, he would pop back in to see how I was getting on. To my surprise, he was genuinely impressed.

"You've done well to get that far; it took me ages," he admitted. "Have you played this before?"

"No," I said. "I've never played a game like this."

Truthfully, I'd never been interested in video games or fairground games. I was only drawn to this one because, for once, my brother had shown me a bit of affection by asking if I wanted to play. It was strange, but because there was no pressure, no scoring, and no one judging me, I was able to relax and let my natural ability come through. Though I wasn't really aware of it at the time. After a while, Tim came back in and decided he wanted to play again now that I'd got so far ahead. I think it bothered him a little, seeing how far I'd managed to get.

"You can go away now," he said.

I left the room with a quiet sense of happiness. He might not have shared a doughnut with me, but he'd let me play his game, taught me how to use the controls, and, best of all, told me I was good too.

I felt good just being in that moment. I walked into my bedroom, lay on my bed, and closed my eyes.

Omg, as I round the corner, I can hear footsteps chasing me. I sprint, pushing my legs to move faster, but my ankle twists, a sharp pain shooting through me. Slowing down is not an option, but I have no choice. The footsteps grow louder, closer, and my stomach churns, twisting into knots. It's the same feeling I get when unwanted visitors invade my space. Yes, you guessed it, him. The man with the rotten teeth, an aftershave with a rotten smell that clings to my throat like a bad memory. His soap smells just as vile. He's near. Too near. I feel it. I hate it. But I have always been good at escaping, in my mind, at least. I trip, and a desperate gasp escapes me. His hands wrap around me, cold and unforgiving. This is it. I wait for it to begin. I close my eyes as tight as I can, and I hear his voice. I wait in anticipation of those words, the words which haunt me, "I know you are awake." And then it begins.

My eyes open, and I sigh a big breath of relief. I was having a nightmare. I was safe. I did not have to endure this insanity and gross feeling tonight.

I lay there with normal feelings while tears trickled down my face. I had to sit in the moment again, feeling confused and annoyed at the serial abuse of my life. My tears were making my hair wet as they reached the side of my head and built up like the sea lapping the shore. I wipe them away, not wanting to dwell on the thoughts running through me. I needed to move to silence the thoughts swirling in my mind. Making tea seemed like a simple distraction, so I got up and busied myself with it. Restless, I wandered into my brother's room, but he immediately snapped at me, ordering me to leave. The warmth I had felt earlier, that fleeting sense of love and acceptance, disappeared in an instant. I should have known better. I had overstepped, pushed my luck again, and now I just felt stupid. Seeking refuge, I stepped outside into the garden, hoping the open air would soothe me. Nature had always been my escape, the place I turned to when everything else felt unbearable. I always used nature to take me away from my pain, to heal me, to nurture me, as if my parents had not realised how to do it. I looked at my rabbit, although I felt uninterested really because he was sleeping and not really playful.

The evening air was turning fresher as I pulled a chair from the garden table and sat beneath the tree. I couldn't shake the restlessness inside me. Sitting still felt impossible, so I went indoors to phone Laura. She was the kind of friend who could pull me out of my own head, someone I could talk to without fear of judgement. I needed that now. I needed a distraction, a connection, something to ground me. I wanted to tell her about work, about everything weighing on me. Laura had always listened, always understood, and apart from Dan, she was the only person who made me feel truly seen. But Dan wasn't around tonight, he was out with Mark, and honestly, that was fine by me.

When I saw Dan next, we talked about the future, about me moving in with him, about trying for a baby once I did. We even came up with a plan, one that seemed foolproof. We'd leave my contraceptive pill packet on the side table where my mum could see it, making her think I was still taking it. Later, we'd claim I had gotten diarrhoea, that the pill hadn't worked. Simple. Believable. The perfect excuse. Work, on the other hand, was a mess. I was still stuck at Owen and Owens, exhausted, dragging myself through each day, hating every second of it. It wasn't as bad as Dibden, at least. There, I had been left to figure things out on my own. Here, they explained what I needed to do, though most of it was boring. I would go to other shops, looking at the pricing to compete with them.

Through it all, one thing remained clear, I wanted a baby. More than anything, I believed I could be a good mother. Better than mine, at least. It wouldn't take much to outdo her; all I had to do was talk to my child, show them kindness, and I would already be ahead. But I couldn't ignore the truth. My mother had been an abuse victim, too. She had done what she could with the little she had. Her father had stolen everything from her, her innocence, her choice, even her sense of self. He had taken her virginity, left her scarred in ways I could barely comprehend.

My mother had spoken of it only once, the single time she allowed herself to share the horror of what had

191

happened to her as a child. It had been an ordinary day, just like any other, until evening arrived, and with it, a suffocating sense of dread. Her mother was going out, her twin sister had plans to stay out with friends, and she was to be left alone with her father. She had begged to go along, pleaded not to be left behind, but her mother refused. She feared that her father would try to touch her while her mother was out, but there was no discussion, no room for protest. She was to stay home. Defeated, she retreated to her bedroom, burying herself in silence.

She had felt lost, trapped between sadness and fear, unsure of what to do. Her father had always favoured her, treating her differently from the others. At times, he had been kind, even gentle, but his affection was tainted, twisted into something cruel. He acted as though she belonged to him, as though her body was his to command.

That evening, he made dinner and called her to the kitchen. In that moment, she had allowed herself to believe everything was fine. Maybe he would suggest a walk, as he often did, taking her to the shore to catch crabs, to wade through the water.

Grandad had called twice, but when Mum didn't respond, he opened her bedroom door and said, "Henrietta, you heard me call. Tell me why you think you do not come straight away?" Mum said sorry as she walked out of the bedroom into the hallway, which was very dark, narrow, and too long. She got to the kitchen, although there was no dinner waiting on the table. She was commanded to take off her panties—she was eight—and lie on the table. Henrietta's dad had touched her many times. She knew what was expected of her, and without hesitation, she obeyed. It was easier that way, easier to let her mind drift elsewhere, to erase the thoughts before they could form. If she shut everything out, if she filled the silence with stories of her own making, she could almost pretend she wasn't there at all. Her mind had learned to protect her, to build walls around the horror, replacing it with something else, anything else. But her body still felt it. No amount of pretending could change that. She positioned herself as he wanted, small and silent, ignoring the searing pain, ignoring his voice as he spoke to her.

Henrietta was numb, and when she had come around from her forced trance, which had been her escape from reality, she became aware of the wetness between her legs and the pain which followed. She heard her father say, "Go clean yourself up, you dirty slut." Those words melted her insides into a space she locked away, throwing away the key, never to reveal it. Sitting alone at the table, she shifted slightly, and the cold wetness sent a shiver through her. Looking down, she saw red. Blood had stained her thighs, trailing down her skin, soaking into the wood beneath her. She had no words, only silence and a strange, hollow numbness. Moving on instinct, she walked to the sink, grabbed a cloth, and began wiping the table. The dull throbbing in her stomach made her pause, but she exhaled sharply and continued, her hands trembling as she cleaned away the debris. She didn't know why she was bleeding or when it would stop. Fear gripped her, but it was the kind that sat heavy and unmoving, the kind that made divulging to her mother impossible upon her return. She had bathed, dressed in her pyjamas, combed her hair, and prepared herself for the evening routine as if nothing had changed. But it had. She sat at the same table where her virginity had been stolen, forced to eat, forced to be grateful for the meal prepared for her. That night, she climbed into bed, pulled the covers up to her chin, and made a decision, she would lock the memory away.

She told me about it once. Just once. That afternoon and night spilled from her lips, but after that, she never spoke of it again. The story had been laid bare, and with it, the weight of something too vast, too unbearable. She had shut the cupboard of horrors tight, terrified of what lay inside. She knew if she ever opened that door again, the skeletons would pour out, a relentless tide, and she might never be able to close it. The past would haunt her forever. And so, she chose silence.

So moving in with Dan and having a baby was my escape plan. I wasn't that unhappy at home, but I could feel better. I knew that for sure, and Dan had brought joy into my life too, and I had started to feel free for the first time. I couldn't wait to move in and work on having a baby.

Dan got in from work, and he said, "I had a tip today." I said, "Oh, nice. Did you buy yourself anything nice?" He said, "No, but I got you this," and he pulled a box of chocolates from behind his back. He had spent the whole tip on me. As I took the gift, I drew closer, and I could see that the car he had painted was green as it lined his nose. I giggled and teased him and said, "How about we wash that off in the shower?" He went blank, then he smirked and said, "Okay, let's." I started the shower, and I put my back on the cold tiles, which made me brace myself as I had shivers go down my spine. I was still dressed in my knickers and bra at this moment, and Dan said, "Why have you still got that on?" I responded, "Because I was leaving it for you to remove."

Dan knew I was aroused, which meant he could touch me without triggering the painful memories of my past. The warm cascade of water soaked through my underwear, but in that moment, I didn't care. All I wanted was to kiss my fiancé and show him how much I appreciated the gift of his love, the awareness that I meant the world to him.

I watched as he struggled to get his jeans off, his long legs making the task even more cumbersome. I adored every part of him. His shirt had already been tossed to the floor, and his jeans clung stubbornly to his feet. With a groan of impatience, he sat down, yanking at the fabric, eager to rid himself of the barrier keeping us apart. I could almost hear his heartbeat, rapid and desperate, mirroring the rising urgency. He stood, his underpants still on, and stepped into the shower with me. The space between us seemed to shrink, the steam swirling around us like a veil. My breath grew shallow, my body tense with anticipation. Dan touched my shoulders, his lips trailing slowly up my neck. The way he moved felt different, more romantic and sensual than normal. My nipples were having a tingling sensation at his touch, and a shiver ran through me as warmth spread from deep within. I closed my eyes, letting the moment take over, feeling the heat of his body pressed close to mine.

He ran his hands lightly along my sides, barely grazing my skin, sending a delicate shiver through me. In response, I rubbed his back, my fingers tracing slow, gentle strokes. I felt him tremble beneath my touch, his body subtly shifting, craving more. He met my gaze with anticipation, then playfully pressed a finger to my nose, saying nothing, just watching me, holding me in the warmth of his hands. I wanted to cry with happiness. True intimacy was something I had rarely known. Normally, being this naked makes me feel self-conscious, awkward even. But with Dan, it was different. He made me feel safe in my body. He had a way of accepting me completely and unconditionally. I could feel his arousal, but it wasn't the driving force between us. More than desire, he wanted to make me feel loved, cherished, and respected. Those were emotions I wasn't used to. Yet, as unfamiliar as they were, I knew I could get used to them. His touch sent warmth through me, untainted by the ghosts of my past. I didn't feel the shame or discomfort that had clouded so many of my previous encounters. For once, I felt good.

A slow hunger stirred within me, the need to taste him, to let our tongues meet and move together. As I leaned in, he mirrored me eagerly, our mouths melting into each other. His tongue danced with mine, teasing and exploring. A deep shiver rippled through me, lifting the hairs on my skin and sending tremors to my core. The urgency between us built. Dan turned me around, his movements tender but firm. My breath hitched, knowing what was coming, but I stayed still. His hands slid forward, cupping my breasts, but as soon as I felt his grip, something inside me tensed. I tried to move from the grip. The moment was changing. I was starting to become aware of the sexual encounter now, and I felt a familiar numbness rising in me.

The thoughts were stirring, and I spun around to kiss Dan before I lost the drive I had been surprised to have while so naked.

Dan stopped for a second and took his face away. He asked, "Are you okay?"

I felt shy again. I was turning into a child, and all my sexual arousal was diminishing. I looked away and got out of the shower. I felt numb and annoyed at myself. I hated being fragile. It made me feel so abnormal.

I wanted so much to like my body and to feel at ease while having wild sex. Most of the time, I could, although if the momentum stopped and gave my mind an opening, then the sexual thirst was quenched, and the desire was gone.

I felt awful. I had started this, and now I was the one ending it. I wanted to cry. Dan never made me feel bad; I just did. It was something deep-rooted, something I couldn't explain. I took his hands, kissed him softly, and then led him to the bed. We shagged quickly, more for his relief than mine, more to silence the guilt than to satisfy any real desire. I was used to pleasing others and pushing my own feelings aside. But I did love Dan, at least.

But when sex became the result of a lack of desire or an intrusion from my past, I felt the need to punish myself to fulfil the wish of a man. A strange, silent obligation. I never understood why, only that I had grown used to it. The theft of my own soul had become second nature. And so, I continued. It rarely happened with Dan, but something about being taken from behind had triggered it—the old memories, the lost girl buried beneath years of pretending. She surfaced in moments like this. The damaged girl. The girl I ignored most of the time.

Living together was fun, though. We had settled into our routine, often showering together, enjoying the intimacy of shared spaces. But we weren't alone in the house. We lived with four others. The girl upstairs used to get high on aerosols, and we'd often hear her. There would be muffled voices as she had people over while enjoying the aerosols. Then there was Lan. He made me nervous as he had a habit of handling razor-sharp knives in the kitchen, watching people too closely. I never stayed for long when he was around. Another housemate was an alcoholic whose girlfriend visited most days. And then there was us.

The kitchen was small, with no running water, just an old heater next to the sink, barely enough to wash a few dishes. There was no washing machine, so we had to trek to the launderette when our clothes piled up. At least we had a cooker. And thankfully, the shower was electric. Off the kitchen, the hallway stretched out. The first left led to the bathroom. The second door on the left was ours. Our little space in this strange, chaotic house.

The room was plain, though it had a fireplace, unused and empty. Two teddies sat on the mantel next to Dan's mirror, with his slippers tucked neatly beneath the shelf. He was surprisingly tidy, so unlike me. I had always been messy, but I swore I would change. A large, old-fashioned sash window let in a persistent draft, the gaps too wide to close properly. The house sat on a private road, right in the middle of a council estate. It scared me slightly. My parents had long since left council housing behind. I was four when we moved to this area, and by the time I was nine, Dad had bought his first house. By eleven, he owned a guesthouse.

My childhood had been filled with drama. One evening, my dad's own mother threatened to murder him in front of dinner guests. I remember feeling oddly disappointed by this because, despite everything, she was my favourite nan. She was fun and full of life. She gave us money and sweets, played games, and told terrifying ghost stories just to jump out and scare us. But I adored her.

My grandad, in contrast, was a quiet, gentle man, tall and slim, with a steady presence. I remember the only time he ever told me off. We were on a family holiday in Wales, and I had scolded the dog too harshly, I suppose. Looking back, I think I did it to feel in control in a world where I had none. Sidney never raised his voice, never got angry, not like my father. But that day, he looked at me with quiet disappointment, and it crushed me. I felt ashamed, knowing I had upset someone so kind.

Well, Grandad was dying, and there had been a falling out with Dad, and that night, she appeared. She got out of the car, and we could hear screaming. Dad ordered us to get upstairs. We looked out the window, as curious children would, watching as she ran up and down the road, shouting nasty things about my dad. As she got closer, I noticed the knife in her hand; she was waving it toward our house, poking at the air, and ranting about wanting to take Dad into the forest for a duel. I didn't know how to process it. I loved this woman so much.

It felt like it went on forever. Eventually, I was sent to bed, expected to sleep as if nothing had happened. And, as usual, by morning, no one spoke of it. I was too afraid to ask. After that night, we stopped seeing Nan for the most part, which was heartbreaking. But Laura still visited her, and I won't lie, it made me jealous. I started to believe Nan loved her more, and that thought hurt. I had always felt so loved by her before.

But I told myself my life was going to change. It would be better now; I finally had an escape from home. The flat wasn't perfect, but I never questioned it. It was better than where I came from. Here, I was wanted. I was welcomed. Even when I wasn't working, I felt okay. Even if the drunk man's girlfriend always left her dutch cap in the bathroom, something I found beyond disgusting. I still preferred it. We would eat well, too. We bought biscuits and steak for Fridays, and Findus crispy pancakes were high on the agenda. My dad used to say, "You eat better than I do." When they came around, we would always have chocolate Hobnobs, which he liked.

The funny thing was, our plan was working because every time Mum came around, she said, "I see you're taking your pill." And I would say, "Yeah." I even said, "They are on the table if you want to check." And she replied, "I already have."

I thought, if only you knew, and smirked inside. I would have been scared for her to know the truth. Dad had gotten shirty enough about me wanting to move out in the first place. He hadn't taken the news well, but for the first time, he couldn't really stop me; I had somewhere to go. I didn't need him anymore. I had an escape. Not that I hated my dad. He had been such a good daddy to me in many ways. But he also left me confused. He could be violent, and that contradiction was something I tried not to question.

I wasn't looking to excuse my father's actions, but I'd heard stories about how he would come home to find us alone while Mum was off spending time with Mary, a friend she used to visit before we moved. I suppose it's easy to pass judgement, but the truth is, I loved them both, despite all the hurt. No matter how much pain I had endured, I carried love and peace in my heart. I couldn't allow myself to hate or resent anyone. That was something I learned in time, to let go of bitterness. I realised that harbouring bitterness only led to my own suffering. I often told myself that although my grandad had stolen my childhood, he wouldn't take my future too. Holding on to anger would only keep me stuck, while the rest of the world kept moving forward. Over time, I developed a way to fortify my mind, to focus on the good, to shield myself from the negativity that surrounded me. It was this ability to block out the bad that kept me grounded, even when the world felt confusing.

Chapter 15: Parenting

Through Pain

I was under five when Mum used to leave us alone. I actually thought my sister was my mum, because she was the one who mostly looked after me. I remember once falling into the lido pool in Southampton. I had said "Mummy" under the water as I was sinking. I couldn't swim, and I was just going down. I saw bubbles escaping from my mouth, and it felt horribly uncomfortable in my nose. The next thing I remember was being pulled out of the water, spluttering and coughing as I tried to get the water out of my lungs. My sister, Suzanne, had jumped in after me. She grabbed my ankle and yanked me back to safety. Then she cuddled me, telling me everything was okay. She was only about ten or eleven herself, but to me, she was my mummy. She made me feel loved, in the best way a big sister could. Poor Mum already had enough to deal with, just being married to my dad. She had put up with so much. He had several affairs, he even cheated on her with her best friend. Mum had come home from hospital with my sister, her third child, and found them in bed together. That image never left her, or us.

It was about a month after I moved in with Dan when my period didn't arrive. We had been trying, but neither of us expected it to happen this quickly. One early morning, while I was at work, I suddenly felt dizzy. I told my boss I wasn't feeling well and wanted to go home. She was kind and told me of course I could. I packed up my things, but I had to wait for the bus. It was November and quite cold. I felt emotional for no clear reason, tearful, even. I couldn't quite place what was wrong with me. I didn't usually feel this bad, and there was no real reason to want to cry. Maybe I was just sickening for something, I thought.

The bus took about forty minutes to arrive. Three others had gone past earlier, of course, that was the usual joke in my area. I lived out of the way, about twelve miles from Southampton, in the New Forest. Not many buses served that route, which was always frustrating. It took an hour to get home on the fast bus, but I didn't care right then. I was exhausted. I rested my head against the window, and the vibration of the bumpy road lulled me to sleep. Luckily, I woke up about ten minutes before my stop. The walk from there wasn't far. On the corner of my road, there was a guest house, with a small convenience store next to it. I popped in to buy some sweets to help with my nausea. My legs felt a bit wobbly, but I got what I needed and put a sweet in my mouth straight away. I remembered something Dad had taught us, that eating something sugary helped with sickness. He used to say it on our boat trips to France when we got seasick.

That little tip made me feel slightly better. When I got home, the kitchen was empty. It was still only five o'clock. Even though I had left work early, the wait for the bus and the hour-long journey meant I hadn't actually gained much time. Still, it was better than getting home at seven. I went straight into my bedroom, dropped my things on the floor, got into bed, and fell fast asleep.

I woke up to Dan kissing my forehead. He asked if I was okay, and I said no, I felt awful. He pulled me into a warm cuddle. I told him my period was late, but surely it couldn't be that already. I'd decided to take the next day off too and go to the doctor. I'd called earlier while waiting for the bus, and they told me to bring my first urine sample of the day in for testing. Dan looked at me and asked, "How would you feel if you were pregnant?"

I replied, "Better, to be honest, at least I'd know why I feel so sick."

Then I mentioned that we needed the gas bottle changed because I was freezing; it had run out. He nodded and left the room. I felt a little relieved, not because I didn't want him there, but because I wasn't in the mood for conversation. I felt strange, and I didn't like it.

I drifted back to sleep, and when I next opened my eyes, it was three in the morning. Dan was beside me. He must have thought I needed the rest and hadn't disturbed me. I still didn't feel hungry; I'd only had a few sweets before falling asleep earlier.

By morning, I got up and took the sample bottle with me to the toilet. It was for my first pee of the day. I unscrewed the lid, but I felt like I was about to start before I'd even positioned the bottle. It wasn't very big, and they'd said the sample had to be taken mid-flow. I began to wee, then quickly moved the bottle into place, but the stream was going everywhere, all over my fingers. I wasn't even sure if any was making it into the bottle. It felt disgusting. I pulled the container away, screwed the lid back on, and thoroughly washed both the bottle and my hands.

I wasn't impressed by the experience, having to wee in a such a small container felt awkward and unpleasant.

I placed the sample on the shelf in the bedroom and went to make a cup of tea. Then I got back into bed beside Dan. I was feeling a bit better and told him, "I don't think I'm pregnant. I feel fine today." Still, I was going to take the sample in as the appointment was already made.

He agreed and said, "I need to get ready for work."

"I have made you a cuppa, it's at the side of the bed." I added.

He looked at me

"I can't wait till tonight to find out," he said. "Should I call your work?"

"No," I replied. "I will want to be with you, and if I'm not, that will upset me, so just let me know once I am home."

He cuddled me before getting out of bed. He cupped my face in his hands. "I really love you, baby," he said.

It felt reassuring. I smiled.

"Go, before I attack you and make love to you," I said, giggling.

Even though I pretended everything was fine, I felt nervous. I was only sixteen, and the thought of being pregnant made me anxious. Planning it had seemed easy, but living it, actually going through it, was starting to feel very real. I tried not to dwell on it. I got dressed, had a proper breakfast with fruit and yoghurt, and headed to the doctor's.

I arrived a little early, but the receptionist was quite rude. She couldn't find my appointment on the system.

"I did speak to someone yesterday," I said politely, "and they asked me to bring in a urine sample."

I waited for her to finish typing stuff into the system. She then looked up abruptly and said, "Go take a seat."

I felt a bit shy, but I did as I was told.

The buzzer sounded quite quickly, and all of a sudden, I felt tearful again. What is wrong with me? I thought. I'd never really liked going to the GP, and now, sitting there knowing exactly why I was there, it all felt far more real than I had anticipated. I took a deep breath and stood up from my seat, which had begun to stick to me, I was sweating, though I hadn't noticed until that moment.

"Hello Amanda, I hear you think you may be pregnant?" the doctor said.

I nodded not wanting to confirm with my voice. I almost felt unable to contain myself and waited with baited breath. I wondered what he was doing because he left the room. When he came back his face looked serious yet friendly.

"Well, young lady," he said gently, "it looks like you are going to be having a baby."

I swallowed hard and forced a smile.

"This was obviously not planned," he continued, "and there are ways of ending a pregnancy."

But something stirred in me. My voice came from nowhere, firm and instinctive. I already felt protective, as if a switch had been flicked the moment I'd heard the words.

"No," I blurted out. "I am keeping my baby."

He gave a small nod. "Alright. You will Need to take your top off, so I can check your breasts."

The request made my stomach turn, but I did as asked, trying to distract myself by focusing on a picture on the wall. He commented that my nipples looked suitable for breastfeeding, then asked me to lie flat so he could feel my stomach.

He then said, "Your stomach muscles are too good and I cannot feel the baby at this stage."

I sat up quickly, eager to leave. He must have noticed, as he said calmly, "I'll organise for a midwife to support you through your pregnancy."

"Okay," I replied, turning towards the door. Just as I was about to leave, I paused and looked back.

"Oh, by the way, can being pregnant make you want to cry all the time?"

"Come and sit down," he said kindly.

We talked for a while. He explained what to expect from my hormones and how they might affect my emotions. His words were reassuring and made me feel less frightened. At least now I understood why I'd been feeling so out of sorts. I stood to leave, thanked him for being so helpful, and left, leaving the door open behind me.

I stepped into the car park, breathing deeply, a mix of exhilaration and exhaustion washing over me. The weight of the moment hung heavy as I made my way back to my flat, but I couldn't resist stopping by Mum's place on the way. When I walked in, I spotted Suzanne, my sister, sitting with her daughter Marie, Mum's granddaughter. It wasn't unusual for Suzanne to be there, but today, seeing Marie felt different. It hit me that I needed to tell Mum about what had happened before Dad found out. The thought of them both not knowing felt too overwhelming.

"Mum, I need to talk to you about something," I said, my voice trembling slightly. She turned, a little surprised.

"What is it?" she asked, her voice steady, but I could hear the hint of concern.

"I didn't get my period," I told her, holding my breath, watching her face for any sign of what she was thinking.

There was a long pause, then she snapped, "How many days are you late?"

I hesitated. "I went to the doctor, Mum," I said quietly, watching her face harden. She looked at me, almost impatient.

"I know you've been on the pill. It's probably just late," she replied, brushing it off.

But I couldn't keep quiet anymore. "The doctor tested me, Mum. It's positive."

For a moment, she just stared at me, then muttered under her breath, "Well, what else did you expect?" Her voice was sharp and unkind.

I felt my chest tighten, and she added, "Dad will go mad."

Her words stung, and I could feel tears prickling at the back of my eyes. This was nothing like the comfort I'd hoped for. I could hear Dad's voice in the distance, coming in through the back door, but he didn't come in to say hello. Instead, he was out there, washing his car. Mum continued chatting with Suzanne, making plans about how she was going to tell Dad. Each word she spoke only made me feel worse. Then, without offering me the chance to go with her, Mum went off to the shops with Suzanne. I was left alone, consumed with a mix of fear and regret. It wasn't how I'd imagined this moment at all.

I sat alone in Mum's kitchen, struggling with the thought of Dad being angry with me. I felt low and just wanted to go home, but I wasn't sure how to get out of the bungalow without running into him on the driveway. Still, I knew I had to leave before Mum got back; the idea of her blurting it out in front of Suzanne like some kind of freak show made my stomach turn. I grabbed my coat and thought, That's it. I'll just go and hope I don't have to talk to Dad. I felt a growing urgency, knowing I needed to leave quickly. As the door shut behind me, I paused and took a breath. I'd have to say goodbye to him, but I was scared of how my voice would sound, as upset as I was.

I tried to rush past him, but he called out, "Hey!"

"I'm just off, bye," I said hurriedly.

"What's up with you?" he snapped, his voice sharp.

I turned to face him, tears already welling. My throat tightened. "Come here, Mandy," he said, softening. "What's wrong?"

Something inside me gave way. I suddenly needed to tell him, better to face his reaction now than have Mum break the news in front of someone else.

I looked him straight in the eye, my tears now falling freely. My voice cracked and trembled as I sobbed, "I'm pregnant, Dad."

What happened next caught me completely off guard.

He stepped forward and wrapped his arms around me, holding me so tightly I could hardly breathe. "My darling girl," he said, "this isn't something to be upset about. It just shows you're becoming a woman."

He pulled away, looked directly into my eyes and said, "Whatever you decide to do, your mum and I will support you, no matter what."

I clung to him, sobbing uncontrollably. Every fear and worry I'd carried about telling my parents poured out in that moment. I had been terrified of Dad's reaction, but it was Mum who had been the harsh one.

"Okay, I'd better go," I said, trying to pull myself together.

"No," Dad replied. "Let's have a cuppa. Stay and tell your mum when she's back."

"She already knows," I admitted. "She was just waiting to tell you, and that's what scared me."

He pulled me close again. "Don't be silly. I'm proud of you, my love."

For the first time, I felt a sense of reassurance. Peace washed over me, and suddenly, I couldn't wait to tell Dan.

I decided to stay at my parents' house until I knew Dan would be home. Now that Mum and Dad were okay with the pregnancy, it felt safe. But the truth was, even though it had been planned, I was still frightened. I knew the weight of what lay ahead, the responsibility, the change, and the need to give my child the best life. My excitement was real, but so was my apprehension. Time dragged. I couldn't wait to share the news with Dan. I was sure he'd feel the same.

When I finally returned home, I went straight to the bedroom, unsure if Dan was in. We didn't have a car, and although he could drive, he'd been banned before we met, that's why Mark always did the driving when Dan visited the garage. I burst into the room holding my breath to try and stop the extreme intensity of my having this news and wanting to share it with the man who showed me love. Dan had wanted the baby as much as me. On opening the door my heart sank because the room was empty.

How could I contain myself another minute. Seconds felt like hours and minutes felt like decades. I was always a very excitable girl. I lay on the bed waiting. When I felt Dan tapping me, I realised I had fallen asleep and thought I should have asked to doctor if there something wrong because I was always so tired lately.

"Come on," he said softly, "what was the result?"

I smiled straight up and he said, "Judging by your smile, I think we have a baby on the way."

I nodded and as I rose up, he flung his arm around me and said, "Okay, I will have to sort myself out now.

I said, "My parents took it okay, and they said something about coming around on Wednesday night for a chat." It was Monday now so at least we had time to ourselves before that. His face dropped and then said, "Have they mentioned why they want to chat?"

I shrugged. "Not exactly. Dad kind of asked if I'd considered not keeping it, but he phrased it like, 'Whatever you want to do, we'll support you'."

"To be honest, Dan, I was terrified of telling him today… but he was the one who made me feel good about it. He was the dad I remember, the one who used to make things right. I was so grateful for that."

"I thought you might have waited for us to tell them together," he said quietly. "Not that I mind. I just didn't expect you to go through that alone, knowing your dad's temper, that you've told me about."

I smiled at his thoughtfulness and hugged him tight.

214

"Have you thought about money, Mandy?" he asked.

I hadn't even given it a second thought and now somehow, I felt ashamed having completely over looked such a massive thing.

"Don't worry," he said. "It will be okay, I will see if dad will help me get into the printing trade.

He looked at me saying, I have everything I ever wanted in you, and now a baby. I want to provide for us."

I suddenly realised that visiting Dan's parents was going to be a big step too. I had only met them once before. They lived on a ten-acre farm in Leamington Spa, Warwickshire. When I met them, they seemed really nice. Although I remembered Dan being a bit of a nightmare on the train journey up there, teasing me the whole way. He kept going on about how scary his parents were and how they owned vicious dogs. At first, I didn't believe him, but I wasn't entirely sure either. There was a tiny part of me that wondered if he might be right. Dan always loved to wind me up, and truth be told, I was just as bad. We had that kind of relationship, laughter was always our thing.

Anyway, as it turned out, the dogs were friendly, and his parents, though a bit strict, were very lovely. His mum didn't hesitate when it came to sorting out the bedrooms. Even though Dan and I were already living together, she made it clear: "As you're not married, of course you'll have separate rooms." I looked at Dan and he shrugged behind her back, pulling a silly face to try and make me laugh.

I was shown to his sister's bedroom, and honestly, I didn't mind. The room felt warm and homely, and I took no offence. If anything, it felt respectful.

The weekend was incredible, even though my parents had always been comfortable with money, these people were on a completely different level. It was obvious in every detail. From the moment we woke up, everything felt so formal yet relaxed, a world away from what I was used to. I started to understand why Dan was always so neat and organised; it was a product of his background. After a delicious cooked breakfast, which was absolutely fantastic, we all settled in, and his parents went about their day. His father was outside, fixing fences, definitely more than just pottering around, to be honest. I found myself wondering where Dan had gone, and suddenly, his mum spoke up.

"I think he's helping his dad with the fences," she said, almost as though she'd read my mind. It felt odd, like she could hear my thoughts. Weird, I thought, but I didn't question it.

"US girls will go out for elevenses," she said. I didn't know what elevenses was, but I didn't dare refuse because I wanted her to like me.

They had two cars. His dad drove a top-of-the-range Saab as a company car, and his mum had a brand-new Volvo, also top of the range. Apparently, we were going to Marks & Spencer to pick up some groceries. She also mentioned a cake outlet and elevenses again. I just nodded and went off to take a shower, hoping I might bump into Dan to ask if he was coming along. I hadn't yet realised that wasn't an option. After showering and getting dressed, I came downstairs to find her waiting with her handbag and car keys. "Shall we go then?" she asked brightly.

I hadn't seen Dan at all, and I was starting to feel nervous, not because of her exactly, but because I felt out of my depth. I didn't know this woman. She was incredibly posh, and I felt... well, a bit stupid. I hesitated and said, "Shall I go say goodbye to Dan first?"

"No, no. They're busy, leave them be, or we'll be delayed."

I took a deep breath, actually, two in quick succession, the sort you take when you're trying to calm your nerves. The silence as we drove off felt awkward, so I started making small talk, commenting that I liked her car. Then I mentioned Hannah, the owner of the bedroom I was staying in. Well that was a diamond of topic because I couldn't shut her up after that. Hannah this and that and how she was in Ireland teaching horse riders and working with jockeys bla bla bla.

By the time we got to Marks & Spencer, I felt like I knew more about Hannah than I did about Dan. It became clear to me that Hannah was the favourite. Still, it was nice to have so much to chat about, and I began to feel more at ease. I made sure to mind my P's and Q's. My parents would

217

have been proud, I thought. In a strange way, I was enjoying her company. She was a little portly and clearly loved her food. She'd eaten a big breakfast followed by toast with half a pot of jam, and now, I'd learnt that elevenses meant tea and cake. At the shop, she loaded up on biscuits and all sorts of goodies.

When she asked me what cake I wanted, I felt embarrassed. I didn't know her well enough to be choosing cake. "I don't mind," I said, smiling politely.

She said, "You need to speak up when you're here. Now, which cake?"

Oh my God, I thought. She was quite forceful, but in a nice way. She was actually trying to include me and treat me. It's just that I wasn't sure how to act. My own parents had been so changeable over the years; I never quite knew what to expect from others. I hadn't expected her to be so direct. In a strange way, she reminded me of my dad.

After our elevenses and a brief food shop, we headed home. Oddly, I felt relaxed with her, even though I barely knew her. She was opinionated, yes, but I found I quite liked that about her.

She was a woman who didn't tolerate any nonsense from anyone, someone who knew exactly what she wanted and commanded respect. It was something I had never been taught, how to respect myself. I found myself admiring her, even aspiring to be like her. She was kind, but also a force to be reckoned with. My mum, on the other hand, seemed to let everyone walk all over her, except when it came to us children. I would hear her agree to things, only to complain later about having to do them. It frustrated me; I couldn't stand it. To say yes so freely, then moan about it afterwards, just didn't seem fair.

I knew Hannah, Dan's mum, wouldn't say yes unless she truly meant it. At least when she agreed to something, she wouldn't become resentful or bad-mouth the person afterwards. I preferred that. I wanted to learn to say no, like that, to have boundaries without fear.

As we made our way down the driveway, which must have been at least a mile long, she asked me what I wanted for dinner. I instantly felt uncomfortable. How was I supposed to know what the options were? Had she already planned some meals? I started to panic, suddenly feeling insecure.

I uttered quietly, "I honestly don't mind, I eat anything."

She cut me off abruptly saying, "That's no use to me, is it?"

I fell silent, feeling awkward. I suppose she had a point, even if it stung. My parents were very different; they never asked me what I wanted. I was never given choices, so I wasn't used to thinking for myself like that. I'd always just done what I was told, ate what was put in front of me, and tried to please people to keep the peace. That was how I stayed comfortable, by making sure I didn't upset anyone.

When we pulled up to the house, I noticed another car parked next to hers that I didn't recognise.

Inside, we went through the boot room and could hear people talking in the kitchen. The dogs were outside. Conny, a deerhound, was tall and slender, still a puppy, though already towering at nearly four feet high. Lilly, the old English sheepdog, was shy and slow now at ten years old. They were both friendly, but not quite how Dan had described them to me.

Sandra had come to see her horse, Bunty and had come in to have a drink because my Dan had offered her one. Bunty was liveried there, and although Hannah was away in Ireland, Dan's parents had agreed to continue feeding and turning the horse out. Riding, however, was Sandra's responsibility now. Sandra was slim, with curly, dark blonde hair. It was a bit odd that they had named their second and third children after themselves; it made things confusing at times.

She greeted us warmly as we entered. Hannah introduced me, saying, "This is Dan's new girlfriend."

Sandra smiled and said, "Nice to meet you." She seemed lovely. I smiled back, though I felt a bit awkward. Seeing Dan there eased my nerves. He smiled at me, clearly sensing my discomfort. He wasn't one to challenge his mum, she had a way of getting her own way, and he knew it.

I slipped past everyone and went upstairs. The kitchen was busy, and I needed a break. I lay on my bed, enjoying a rare moment of peace. As lovely as everyone had been, I'd found the whole weekend overwhelming.

Constantly worrying about what to say or how to behave had been exhausting. I heard footsteps on the stairs and hoped it was Dan. I walked to the door, pretending I was going to the bathroom, just to check.

There he was, smiling at me, giggling as he came closer. When he reached me, he slipped his arm around me and asked if I wanted to go for a walk. He knew I was feeling overwhelmed and needed a moment to myself. He was always so thoughtful.

"Yes," I said diving on him and kissing him quick before getting caught. Feeling like a naughty school girl.

Despite the ups and downs, it had been a lovely weekend. But I knew that telling his parents about the baby was going to be difficult. They were kind, but wanting their son to have a child at this stage was a different matter entirely. Strangely enough, I thought my parents might react worse, though they'd started to come around to the idea.

Dan said, "I will go call my mum and let her know. Shall we walk to the phone box together?"

I nodded, and we held hands as we left the flat and walked down the gravel track. The phone box was about a mile and a half away, but we both enjoyed walking, especially hand in hand. When we got there, I started feeling hungry, which wasn't ideal. Hunger made me nauseous during pregnancy. Thankfully, there was a convenience shop next door, so I popped in and got a sausage roll, which I began eating straight away.

"I'll wait outside," I told Dan. Phone boxes were cramped and smelt funny. I needed the fresh air and food to settle my stomach.

I could hear Dan talking to his mum. He sounded calm, no signs of tension or stress. I heard him say, "I'll sort it out," a couple of times, and then, "I'll chat to Dad later."

When he came out, he looked fine. "Well, that's done," he said.

"Were they upset?" I asked.

"They didn't seem it," he replied.

By that point, we had started opening each other's mail. A week later, Dan received a letter, addressed just to him, but I didn't think twice about opening it. He'd often asked me to open his post before, and I'd grown used to doing it now

Well until now; I started reading the letter.

Dear Son, after seeing this I felt I should stop reading because his dad had written to him personally. I put the letter back into the envelope and put in on the mantelpiece for Dan to read it. Although I felt a strange pull to know what was being said and my pregnancy hormones were not being kind.

I spent a while just walking around, trying to pass the time. With hours to go before Dan came home, I couldn't settle. It was only ten in the morning, and I hadn't gone into work because the morning sickness had been unbearable. Yet, at that moment, sickness wasn't the issue; it was the growing anxiety about what that letter contained.

The wait was making me restless. In an attempt to distract myself, I decided to head over to Mum's. I had no money, so walking the two miles felt like a better option than just waiting. Anything to avoid staring at the letter. I knew Dan would let me read it anyway, but the waiting was starting to feel unbearable.

Mum was in the kitchen when I walked in; she had just returned from the bakery. They were having lardy cake, which I'd always thought was rather disgusting. My sister was there, along with Marie, which was nice. It felt good to be away from the flat and the letter; it gave me something else to think about for a while. Dad came in saying, "Get that lardy cake cut and the kettle on, I am looking forward to this." They had apparently gone to Romsey, where dad insisted they do the best lardy cake he had ever tasted. My parents loved their sweet treats and always liked to indulge. They used to get really excited about food. I'd never been that fond of cake myself; I'd always preferred savoury things. But with this little human growing inside me, that was starting to change.

Mum made Suzanne a coffee, and I suddenly had to run to the toilet to throw up. I had discovered that the smell of coffee and cooking mincemeat made me violently ill. It wasn't just nausea, it was projectile vomiting. When I came back to the table, Dad offered me a piece of cake. I felt fine for about ten minutes before the sickness returned. I tried desperately to stop myself being sick, but my mouth began to water, and as soon as I tasted the saliva, I knew it was coming. The vomit rose into my throat, and I hated it. The lumps made me feel like I couldn't breathe, and it carried on for so long I genuinely felt like I might die. I went to the sink to wash my face and glanced at my reflection in the mirror. I was horrified, my face was covered in red marks. The strain of vomiting had burst the tiny blood vessels under my skin, leaving me looking awful.

I returned to the kitchen but soon realised I needed to leave. The nausea was overwhelming, and I couldn't ignore it any longer. I apologised and explained that I needed to go home to rest. Dad, noticing how unwell I looked, offered me a lift, and I gratefully accepted. As we drove down the road, I felt the familiar wave of sickness rise again. "I need to say goodbye, Dad," I muttered, struggling to hold it in. "I'm going to be sick." Dad glanced over at me, concern in his eyes, asking if I'd be okay. I just shook my head and hurriedly said, "I'm going to be sick. Bye."

I dashed inside, not even pausing to say another word, and rushed straight to the toilet. After I was done, I remembered the dried biscuit the GP had suggested during my first antenatal visit. I had mentioned my struggles with keeping food down, and he had recommended trying it to ease the nausea.

I fell asleep, and when I woke up, I felt much better. At some point, I'd woken again, been sick, and gone back to sleep. Now it was four o'clock, and I made myself a cup of tea. My eyes drifted back to the letter. The suspense was becoming too much.

I walked over and grabbed it, and lay on the bed to read it.

Dear Son,

I want you to know how proud we are of you. You have had your problems in the past although you seemed to have sorted yourself out now.

As I read those words, I was feeling bad because it was just his dad telling him he was proud. I felt wrong for reading something so personal. I turned the page to see if there was anything on the back and the words turned me cold with fear.

In this day and age, son you do not have to stay with this girl. You can run away and not have anything to do with her ever again. You do not have to be responsible for this child.

I wished I hadn't read it. I felt horrified. What was I supposed to think! His dad was basically advising him to leave me pregnant. I didn't know how to feel. I was so angry with his dad. It felt like he hated me.

I folded the letter and slipped it back into the envelope, placing it quietly on the mantelpiece. I didn't want to look at it again. I was shocked by his dad's words, appalled, really. My own father had said he'd support any decision we made. He'd never once suggested I run, or abandon my responsibilities. Yet here was Dan's dad, doing just that. I didn't know how to feel, and worse, I didn't know how to tell Dan I'd read the letter. I felt worse now than when I was throwing up. What on earth had I just read? What kind of man tells his son to walk away from a child? I was stunned. Maybe they had money, but clearly, money didn't come with moral values.

I started to feel deeply awkward. What was I going to say when Dan got home? I almost wished I could unread it. I already struggled with feeling unwanted, and this certainly didn't help. It felt like I'd been waiting hours for him. Finally, I heard the door handle turning. My heart started to race, making the nausea worse.

I looked up, unsure of what expression I wore, but Dan's face shifted the moment he saw me. It was as if he could read my thoughts. I swallowed hard as he asked, "You okay?"

I nodded, not trusting myself to speak, because the truth would have to be a lie. I had hidden the letter. I didn't want to upset him or make a scene. But inside, I was hurting. It broke my heart to feel so rejected, rejected not just as a person, but as the mother of his child. I was used to rejection. I'd felt unworthy before. But I swore this baby wouldn't experience the same. That letter had made me angry, but I didn't want that anger spilling onto Dan.

We kissed and cuddled. He asked how I was feeling. I told him how rough it had been, that I'd been sick four times, had gone to my parents' house, and had to come back because I felt so ill. But I reassured him I was feeling a bit better now.

The evening went quick after we had dinner, I felt ready to tell him about the letter.

"Dan, I am so sorry, I read your letter today."

"Why are you sorry? You know I don't mind you reading my letters, there is never anything very exciting in the post."

"Well… it's from your dad," my voice went to a slow stutter.

He looked confused. "Why did he write to me? What does he want? That's unusual. What did he say?"

"I think you should read it," I replied, taking the letter and popped it in his hands and kissed him on the cheek.

"I'll leave you alone to read it and go for a walk." I went to open the door and he grabbed my hand. "Anything my dad has to say is said to us. We are a team. It's you and me. It's our family now."

I shrugged and said, "Please, I need some fresh air." Although in truth I didn't want to read his expressions while reading those words. I couldn't bear to see his reaction. I hadn't once considered that Dan might leave me; we both knew this baby wasn't an accident. We had planned for this little life. It was his dad who hadn't been let in on the truth.

227

The thought of seeing the disappointment in Dan's eyes, the man I loved, was almost unbearable. The idea that his father's words could cause him such pain stirred something deep inside me, anger mixed with an overwhelming sense of sickness. I could feel the weight of the injustice, knowing Dan was left to endure that hurt alone. The tears started again, and this time, they weren't just from sadness but from a deep ache, a turmoil I couldn't shake. How was I going to face him when we met again? I didn't hold a grudge; it wasn't who I was but this felt different. It felt like a direct rejection of something so precious to me, of our baby, and that just didn't sit right. It hurt in a way I couldn't explain.

I quickly wiped my tears as I heard footsteps approaching. I'd lingered too long in the front garden, and now I could hear someone walking faster towards me. My heart pounded with anxiety; I didn't want him to see how hurt I truly was. I took a deep breath, forcing a smile as I turned around.

"Sorry you had to read that darling… the man is out his mind. How dare he"

Dan's voice trembled with anger, and he started swearing, which only made me feel worse. I didn't want to be the cause of tension between him and his dad. I had experienced enough pain from feeling unwanted by my own parents, I certainly didn't want Dan going through anything similar because of me.

"Hey… look. It must have been a shock for him. He was just thinking of you. It's a complement."

A flipping compliment. I couldn't believe I'd just said that.

"Well at least he cares," I said.

But as the words left my mouth, I felt the sudden surge of nausea. I didn't even explain, I just bolted past Dan, heading straight to the bathroom. He must've thought I was running from him, but I could barely think at all.

The vomiting came in waves, relentless and violent. I couldn't breathe between retches. My throat burned and my nose stung from the acidity. It smelt like coffee, bitter, black coffee, and the taste clung to the back of my throat. I hated it. I felt drained, both physically and emotionally. Everything about the moment felt cold, like we had argued, like something had gone wrong between us.

When the sickness finally eased, I brushed my teeth, though the bitter taste lingered. At that point, I didn't care about the stupid letter. I just wanted comfort. I needed to feel safe again. As I stepped out of the bathroom, Dan was walking down the hallway toward me.

"Hey, come here. You must be feeling rubbish," he said gently lifting my chin for me to reach his gaze as he was so tall.

"Oh, that letter," I muttered, the words catching in my throat.

"No. Let's forget the letter. I am more worried about you throwing up like this."

"I must admit, I am getting worried now myself because I can't cope with this."

"Shall I make you a doctor's appointment for tomorrow?" he asked.

"I am not sure really. I have an antenatal the next day, I'll wait for that," I replied.

Dan nodded, though I could tell he wasn't convinced. Still, he didn't press it. That evening passed calmly. We lay together on the bed, and he stroked my back gently. Eventually, I drifted off to sleep in the comfort of his presence.

Chapter 16: A Voice Reclaimed

The next day, when Dan got home from work, he told me my parents were planning to come over. I'd gone to the shop earlier to buy my dad's favourite biscuits, though I felt nervous about their visit. I couldn't explain exactly why, but something unsettled me. I kept it to myself, I didn't want to worry Dan. We had just finished dinner when I heard voices outside, followed by a knock at the door. I opened it to find my mum standing there.

"How did you get in?" I asked.

"There was a man in the kitchen who let us both in," she said.

"Oh, that would be Lan."

"Yes, maybe. He seemed very polite."

"Well, you obviously didn't see Lan then," I muttered under my breath.

"Yes, he introduced himself to us and told us to go through."

"Well, I am lucky if he looks at me, let alone speaks to me… anyway come in. Do you want a cuppa?"

"I recon you know the answer to that," Dad said.

231

Mum followed me into the kitchen saying she would help me make the tea. I was hoping she wouldn't although I didn't much fancy being alone with Lan either.

"Okay, you can put the kettle on then," I said.

I gave a half-laugh, more out of nerves than amusement. The anticipation of what this conversation would be about was starting to get to me. I'd had a couple of days to dwell on it, and Dan and I had talked it through too, but we couldn't figure out what they wanted to discuss. We knew it was about the baby, but beyond that, we were stumped. They'd already shown they were willing to support our decision, so why did they need to speak with us so soon?

Mum finished making the tea and I had managed to get out of the chore altogether as I needed to pee desperately. I seemed to be in the toilet either peeing or throwing up nowadays.

"You managed to get out of that, didn't you?" she said with a smile.

I laughed and rushed ahead to open the door for her, as her hands were full. She had taken Lan's tray, so I knew I needed to return it quickly. I didn't want to give him any reason to be off with me. Once I'd returned the tray, I re-entered the room, and instantly felt the atmosphere shift. It was quiet. Too quiet. That wasn't normal for my parents. What the heck is this about? I wondered.

A strange tension filled the air. I could feel my internal organs tightening, causing cramp in my stomach. I stood to stretch it out, unable to sit still with the discomfort.

"Sit down. We have something to say," Dad's voice sounded calm, even so I was really wondering what was coming. I glanced briefly at Dan as I siddled down beside him wanting not to feel alone.

The silence was torturous. I felt like Dad was trying to summon the courage to speak. My mouth began to water, and I fought the growing nausea. I felt dizzy from the intensity of it all.

"Your mother and I have been chatting, and we know you want to keep the baby. We were wondering if you wanted to get married."

"NO," I said without much thought.

Yes, I wanted the baby, that was never in question. But marriage? I was sixteen. I hadn't even considered it. I loved Dan, of course, and I saw us together forever. But marriage now? No. We were engaged, but that had always felt symbolic, a token of commitment, not a formal plan. I had thought we'd get married later, once we were settled and I had a job.

Dan looked at me, startled. I stood abruptly and walked out, pretending I needed the toilet. I just needed space to think. I shut the door and leaned against it. I was furious. How dare they try to control me again? I had left home, and still they were meddling in my future.

When I returned, I tried to steer the conversation elsewhere, but Dad wasn't done.

"Well, we want you to know if you change your mind we will pay for your wedding. We are offering because we know you couldn't afford it yourself so as long as you know. The offer will stand forever."

I smirked and said, "Who fancies a biscuit."

"Okay, I will have one if you have the chocolate hobnobs," Dad said.

"Me too," Mum uttered.

The mood eased slightly, and thankfully the conversation moved on. Still, I was relieved when they left. The whole evening had felt intense, and unnecessary.

But just when I thought it was over, it happened.

"Why not get married Mands?" Dan asked gently.

For goodness' sake, I thought. How do I get out of this now. I was pregnant with his baby do I have a right to deny him marriage?

I said, "Please let's leave it, I don't think it's a good idea. It would look like a gunshot wedding! I want to marry because we thought of it, not because my parents brought it up." I hadn't raised my voice to Dan before, but I felt annoyed at his thoughtfulness. Did he really think getting married was going to make it better or easier.

I was so cross with my parents because now Dan and I were having our first dispute because of them and their interference. I was seething mad.

I started to feel the same way I had all my life, like I had to do things to please everyone else. And here it was again. My life, my body, my baby, but other people calling the shots. Still, I knew I was being unfair to Dan. I reached out, took his hand, and asked for a cuddle.

"I am sorry. It's just I wasn't expecting this and I need to stop the discussion if you don't mind. It's not you," I explained. "It just feels like my parents are taking over yet again. Can we talk later?"

"Yeah, okay," he replied and the topic was changed but we went straight to sleep without much chatting. Although we had cuddled and it felt okay and comfortable still. In the morning, Dan was already in the kitchen when I woke. I joined him, but as I walked in, he turned to me and asked again if I'd marry him. Yes, we were already engaged. But we'd never discussed doing it now. It was starting to feel like pressure. I blamed my parents, they'd planted the idea, and now Dan couldn't let it go. I knew I wanted to marry him someday. Just not now.

And yet, for the rest of the week, Dan kept bringing it up. I couldn't bear to keep rejecting him. I loved him so much. So, eventually, I said yes. We called my parents, and they arranged to come round the following week to discuss the details. The idea of planning a wedding sent chills through me. I loved Dan, I truly did, and I knew I wanted a life with him. But it all felt so rushed.

My parents came round to start planning the wedding, and before I knew it, they had even settled on a few dates. One of them was Valentine's Day, so we decided on that. It was all a bit much for me, and I let them take charge of the arrangements. Mum and Dad seemed pleased, busying themselves with the details. The winter passed quickly, mostly because I was with Dan, and that made everything feel easier. Pregnancy, on the other hand, wasn't getting any easier. Work was becoming more exhausting, and I was always tired. By January, I was starting to show, though I wasn't sure how much of it was baby-related. I had to eat constantly just to keep the nausea at bay. I remembered the GP's advice: if I sat quietly in bed with a dry biscuit, it helped keep the sickness at bay. It didn't always work, but it often did. I'd grown accustomed to being sick now, and it was a daily routine, four or five times a day. Sometimes it was just bile, and it tasted like very strong coffee, clinging to the back of my throat. The aftertaste would linger for hours.

Although I was happy, Dan and I had settled into a routine, and curling up with him at the end of the day felt amazing. For the first time, I felt like I had finally made it; peace reigned. We had a schedule of sorts: different things on different nights, and Saturday was launderette day. That was the annoying part; we had to walk almost two miles down the road, lugging heavy black bags full of washing. This led to our first real disagreement, our first proper argument. Dan snapped at me to hurry up, and I took it badly. I was pregnant and exhausted, and the bag was heavy for me. I dropped it on the pavement and stormed off. Yes, it was dramatic, but my hormones were raging, and I needed to make a stand. In hindsight, Dan couldn't have carried both bags, they were massive. He dropped his and came running after me, apologising. We made up and agreed that we wouldn't let the laundry pile up so much again. From then on, we'd go more frequently. Not long after that, Dan got a letter saying he would be getting his driving licence back. We immediately started saving for a car. It was such a relief. We'd both been quietly worrying about how we would manage once the baby arrived, especially without transport. The baby was due on 18th July, and he'd have his licence back in April, perfect timing. Things had a way of working out. Most of our arguments, or little niggles, were about chores. We were still kids really, learning how to live together and manage a household. Dan was getting excited about the wedding, and I'd smile and say the right things, but inside I didn't feel the same. I wanted to be with him, but I also wanted my own identity, my own special wedding when I was mature enough to plan it myself and pay my own way.

Whenever I visited my parents, Mum would always bring up the wedding. What was strange was how she had started to show her affection now that I had moved out. She was getting excited about it all, and even Dad was too. It felt like now that I was gone, they had begun to appreciate me. In hindsight, I suppose it was because life had become easier for them. They had more time, more resources, and weren't caught up in the chaos of day-to-day parenting anymore. I hadn't seen that growing up. That week, I had a dress fitting. Mum had decided there was no point looking too early since the baby was growing, so we arranged to go dress shopping four weeks before the wedding. She picked me up and we went to a local bridal shop. "We'll hire the dress," she said, "you'll never wear it again." I couldn't really disagree, it was her money, after all.

So I agreed and walked into the shop. In that moment, I felt a flicker of something. I was being treated well, being made to feel special. My sister had come along, and they were offered champagne. Even though I was underage and pregnant, the lady offered me one too. I declined, of course. I wasn't going to put anything into my body that could harm my baby. I was becoming more maternal with each passing day.

I must have tried on every dress in the shop before we found it, or rather, Mum and Suzanne found it. Don't get me wrong, I didn't hate it, but it wouldn't have been the dress I'd have chosen if I were in control of my own destiny. Still, I smiled and nodded. It was just a dress. My body was changing so quickly that I didn't feel attractive anyway. But Dan didn't seem to care. The shop assistant said to come back the week before the wedding for measurements, and they'd do the alterations there since she was a seamstress. Mum was horrified, what if the dress wasn't ready? I didn't share her concern. Perhaps the benefit of not being emotionally invested in the wedding was that I had zero stress about it. I honestly couldn't have cared less what I wore. I'd have walked down the aisle in a white tablecloth if someone had asked. Now they were planning a hen do too. They'd decided on a local pizza place. It felt more like something for Mum and Suzanne than for me. I couldn't have cared less about it.

Although I was happy going along with it. I had enjoyed being included for once in their chats well not all the time. I felt less left out than usual. Let's put it that way. Now their chats turned to my hen do, although in all fairness it had nothing to do with me. Not once did I get asked about what I had wanted and I think my sister was inviting her fiends too. I didn't care I just went along with it. I had what I wanted I had my baby growing in my stomach, my piece of gold. My love of my life who I felt closer too each and every day. I would place my hand over my stomach and chat to her. I wanted a girl and so in my mind it was my daughter. We had been chatting about names Dan and I although we couldn't agree on a boy's name at that time. Although the girl was going to be call Jennifer after my favourite auntie my mums twin sister who was amazing, I had always felt very close to her.

Sometimes, when I spoke to my unborn baby, I would call her Jenny. I couldn't feel her move yet; she hadn't started kicking. At times, I even questioned whether there really was a baby inside me. The constant vomiting was the only reminder that I was, indeed, pregnant. Then one morning, it happened. I woke up with a pain in my stomach. Dan had already left for work, and I decided to call in sick. A wave of fear swept over me; I had a horrible feeling something wasn't right. My stomach just didn't feel normal. I went to the bathroom, brushed my teeth, and decided I would go to Mum's. I wasn't well enough to walk, so I planned to take the bus. I didn't want to be on my own that day. Deep down, I was scared, terrified that something might be wrong with the baby. As I was about to leave the house, I felt a sudden urge to pee. I rushed back indoors and sat on the toilet. Then I looked down. My knickers were red. My heart froze. I stared at the blood, willing it to disappear. Fear gripped me. Was I losing my baby?

I just wanted to be at Mum's already. I needed answers. When I wiped myself, I saw no blood on the tissue, which gave me a small glimmer of hope. Still, I didn't understand why I had bled at all. I went back into the bedroom, changed into fresh knickers, and hurried for the bus. Thankfully, I hadn't missed it. At Mum's, Suzanne was there with her sister-in-law and her baby. I asked them both what it meant to bleed during pregnancy. Shirley looked up and said, "I bled with this little one, and here she is, right in front of you. Just take it easy and rest for a couple of days." Suzanne added, "It'll probably be fine." That reassurance meant everything to me. I trusted my sister like gospel; her words settled me completely. I decided to take the rest of the week off work. When I went to the toilet at Mum's, there was no more blood, but I dreaded every trip to the bathroom. Each time I pulled my knickers down, I did so with squinted eyes, silently praying I wouldn't see red again. I had never felt such fear. I'd faced so much in life, but this, this was truly terrifying. I had grown to love the baby inside me in a way I had never loved myself. The bond felt fierce and strong. I wanted to protect her. I wanted to be the best for her. But a part of me also feared letting her down. The day passed quickly. My stomach had settled somewhat, and although I was sick twice while at Mum's, that was nothing unusual by now.

As I waited for the bus home, I felt the need to pee again. There were no toilets around, so I had to wait. I'd started needing to pee more frequently, even waking up in the middle of the night for it. If I wasn't peeing, I was throwing up. I was sleeping more, always tired, and feeling incredibly emotional. Despite it all, I was happy. Happy that this little being was growing inside me. When I got home, I

240

noticed I had bled again, though it was lighter than before. I waited anxiously for Dan to return. I needed to share this with him; I felt so lonely. The "what ifs" plagued my mind, filling the space with fear. Yes, we could try again if the worst happened, but I had already fallen in love with this baby. I cherished her. Losing her would shatter me. I was eleven weeks and five days pregnant, and this was the happiest I had ever been. Could life really be so cruel? After everything I had endured, would it take this from me too? I had always been someone who accepted the hard things in life. But losing this baby? That was not something I could ever accept. She was the love I had been searching for all my life, already stirring inside me, warming me through the sick days and sleepless nights. The vomiting, the peeing, the fatigue, it was all worth it. She was my little angel. The angel growing inside me.

I lay on the bed and, before I knew it, I had fallen asleep. As usual, Dan's kiss on my forehead woke me. He asked if I was alright, but the look on my face must have said it all; his expression changed instantly, worry etched across it.

I tried to stay strong, but I couldn't hold it together. "I've been bleeding, Dan," I said quietly. "My stomach was aching this morning, and then there was blood in my knickers."

His face dropped. He didn't speak at first but pulled me into his arms. His voice caught slightly as he whispered, "It's going to be alright, Mands. Stay strong." Then, more gently, "Have you continued bleeding, or has it stopped?"

"It stopped while I was at Mum's," I replied, "but it started again later. That's why I came to lie down and rest."

"Then don't go back to work this week," he said firmly. "Stay home and rest. I'll do all the chores."

Dan had already taken on a lot of responsibility. He'd recently fallen out with his dad, who was now refusing to come to our wedding. To help with the expenses, Dan had taken on some of my responsibilities at the garage to earn more money. My dad was furious with Dan's father, he thought it was completely unfair. He even wrote to Dan's parents, saying he was covering all the wedding costs and that he wanted them to be part of this special day. He invited them to stay at our house to make things easier. Hannah replied to Dad's letter. She said that Dan's father had refused to attend, though she was trying her best to change his mind. She added that she hoped they would both be able to come and thanked Dad for his kindness, saying she appreciated him taking care of everything. Dad told us about the letter because he felt Dan had a right to know that his father might not come to his own wedding. But he also reassured Dan that he would support him through it. My parents really liked Dan. He had become a welcome part of the family. Things actually felt nicer at home since I'd moved out. It was as though having Dan made me more acceptable to them. Even Mum had become more chatty lately. Don't get me wrong, she could still hurt my feelings, but she was finally speaking to me like she genuinely liked me. That meant more than I could express. After so many years of feeling isolated and cold-shouldered by her, and after all the shouting, this change felt huge.

It Is Not How Life Starts, It Is How You Finish It

It didn't feel right, seeing him take on all the chores while I rested. I could tell he was doing far too much, and now I was starting to feel guilty about it too. We had dinner together and spent the rest of the evening cuddling. I couldn't help but dread him going to work the next day, worrying about being alone, just in case the bleeding started again. It had been quiet since his return, but I still couldn't shake the fear. I woke up a few times during the night, and each time, there was no blood. Slowly, I started to think that maybe everything would be okay now, but doubt crept in. I wondered if the baby was still alive inside me. The feeling inside me was indescribable, numb, and empty. When I woke up the next day, I felt a strange relief when I didn't see any blood after my first trip to the bathroom. But the worry was still there, hiding just beneath the surface, like a constant companion. Although I hated work, I found myself wishing I could go back. At least it would give me something to focus on, something to distract me from my swirling thoughts. The day seemed to drag on until I finally fell asleep. Lately, it seemed like I could sleep for hours, both day and night. I'd never felt this level of exhaustion before, and it was unsettling.

A week or so passed by and I hadn't bled again. The worry began to ease, and work kept me busy, which helped. Mum and Suzanne were now arranging the hen do and inviting people; around ten were coming. None of them were there for me, but I didn't care.

The wedding plans were consuming every bit of my time now: rehearsals, dress fittings, and the hen night. I hardly knew which way was up. Still, I had grown accustomed to the idea of marriage. After all, it wasn't as if we hadn't made the decision ourselves in the first place. I always tried to stay positive, as it was easier than dealing with the doubts and fears that tried to creep in. Besides, I didn't really have time to dwell on it; there were only two weeks left until the big day.

By this point, I had stopped bleeding, and everything seemed to be going fine. My stomach was beginning to show the unmistakable signs of pregnancy, and it was an exciting feeling. Then, two weeks before the wedding, something happened that I'll never forget. For the first time, I felt something inside me. At first, I thought it was just the usual fluttering, like butterflies, but no. This time, it was different. She kicked me hard. Oh, what a little darling, I thought. It was a moment that made it all real, and suddenly, I wasn't scared anymore. Everything was working out perfectly. Even Dan's dad, who had been somewhat reluctant, had been convinced to come to the wedding. It felt like everything was falling into place.

The hen do took place that weekend. Mum had wanted it out of the way before the final wedding rush began. When I arrived, my sister's friends greeted me warmly; everyone seemed genuinely excited. They asked what I'd like on my pizza. I didn't have much of a preference, so I went with the full meat feast. "Yummy," I thought, "plenty of cheese, please." I added that request to the waitress, who smiled and promised to make sure I got extra. That small gesture made me feel at ease. I was starting to feel more comfortable in this setting, surrounded by laughter and light-hearted chatter. I had finally accepted the moment for what it was. Meanwhile, Dan, Dad, my brother, and his friends had gone into town for a meal of their own. During the evening, I needed to use the toilet. I asked where it was and excused myself. As I sat down, a sudden wave of emotion washed over me, and without warning, I began to cry. Just for a moment, fear crept in. But I quickly composed myself, wiped my tears, and rejoined the group. I didn't think much more of it; by now, I was well aware that hormones could reduce me to tears without warning or reason. The evening went smoothly, and yes, the extra cheese on my pizza did not go unnoticed.

The final dress fitting also came and went. There was hardly anything for the seamstress to adjust. My shape had changed, though not necessarily in size; the baby bump had become more defined. I might have even lost weight from the stress and activity. I barely had time to snack on junk food these days. The sickness was still lingering, but compared to vomiting four or five times a day, one or two felt manageable. The night before the wedding, Dan stayed at the flat while I stayed at Mum's. I slept in my old bedroom, which felt oddly comforting. My sister had moved out by then, so the room was all mine again for one last night. After the wedding rehearsal, which finished at eight, Dan had dinner at Mum's, then Dad drove him back home.

My sister and cousin were to be my bridesmaids. As I looked at them, I thought they looked far better than me, but I didn't mind. I was content. In fact, I was happy. I had begun to feel genuinely positive about the wedding, especially with the baby on the way. Getting married now felt like the right thing to do for her. For Jennifer. She had become my focus. Her, and Dan. They were my world now. The rehearsal dinner had brought people together. Mum had prepared a generous spread: quiches, sausage rolls, and all sorts of finger foods. All homemade, of course. Mum loved cooking and was clearly in her element. People gradually left by nine, which I was secretly grateful for. I was exhausted. The ceremony was set for 3 p.m. the following day, a later time than most weddings, meaning I wouldn't see Dan again until the aisle. I wasn't thrilled about that, but I had a full morning ahead, hair appointments with Mum, my sister, and Lucy at eleven, which would keep me busy. Being pregnant, I rarely woke early anymore, but her kicks were growing stronger by the day. I loved feeling her move inside me, it was reassuring. She was doing well, growing stronger, her little football kicks a daily reminder. At times, I even wondered if she might be a boy, based on how powerful they felt.

Chapter 17: The Gift of Survival

That night, I went to bed both exhausted and excited. I was about to be married. Me, little Mandy, the girl who had once been weighed down with worry and fear. My life had changed so much, it was barely recognisable. And it had changed for the better. This journey taught me something important: we can never predict the future, and sometimes, we just have to trust the path ahead. Yes, it might be stained or imperfect, but things can improve. My life had shifted into something unexpectedly blissful.

I closed my eyes, and the next moment, I opened them to my wedding day. Wow. I thought. Today's the day. I'm getting married, age sixteen years with Dan. And soon, our little bundle of joy will arrive, completing our family. I felt incredibly positive. I knew it was going to be a good day. It was already ten o'clock by the time I woke, though Mum informed me she'd been in three times already. She was practically buzzing. I'd never seen her like this before, jolly, mellow, and full of excitement. In truth, this day was just as much hers as it was mine. She'd planned it all, paid for everything, and made sure each detail was sorted. She deserved her moment. I was genuinely grateful to both my parents for making it all possible. Then I remembered,

Dan's parents were going to be there too. They were picking up Dan and heading to the church together. A flicker of anxiety passed through me. What if his dad tried to talk Dan out of it? But the thought passed quickly. I knew Dan would be waiting at the altar. He loved me. Still, I wondered how his dad would receive me today.

Not that I had anything to feel guilty about. He had been the one in the wrong. But as time went on, I had started to understand his perspective. In his eyes, he was trying to protect his son, and who could fault a parent for that? Besides, the letter he'd written wasn't meant for me. It hadn't been said to hurt me, and it came from a place of concern, not cruelty. For all he knew, the pregnancy was a mistake. He didn't know it was planned. I had forgiven him already, and I was genuinely pleased he had chosen to attend. That morning, as I stood on the edge of something new, I realised just how far I'd come. The traumas of the past were no longer clinging to me. For the first time in years, I felt at home, safe, happy, and healthy. And I was ready. I loved knowing I was about to bring a new miracle into the world. One big, happy family. Having Dan in my life and moving out had really changed the dynamics within my own family, and I rarely thought about the past anymore. Everything was beginning to look so bright and promising. The nerves were definitely kicking in now; even I was starting to feel excited. It was time to get ready for the big day. We were heading to a local hairdresser, and since there were four of us, it would take until one o'clock to get through everyone. The hours seemed to be vanishing before my eyes, and I was starting to worry. I still had to have my makeup done, get into my dress, and have something to eat. Waiting until three o'clock for food at the wedding felt far too late for me, especially with all the photos afterwards, I knew it would be much longer before we actually got to eat.

I took a breather and then shouted, "I'm ready!" Even though, truthfully, I didn't feel ready at all. I wondered if I could get a lift back from someone else rather than wait for the last three to finish. But I was instantly rejected.

"No, we'll all come back together," Mum retorted.

Oh well, I thought, it was just a suggestion, though I felt slightly annoyed. Still, by the time we got there, everything became so busy that time flew by.

I ended up really liking my hair. The stylist took one look at me and said, "I know what will suit you." She worked her magic and I truly did look fantastic. Suzanne was doing my make-up. Mum insisted it was pointless spending extra money, as Suzanne was very good, and we'd had plenty of practice runs. I think Suzanne and I had grown quite close during this time. She felt protective of me, and in truth, all my family dynamics had shifted. I finally felt settled.

Back at the house, things turned chaotic. Everyone was rushing around, and family members began arriving early, just popping round, thinking it would be fine. Mum became visibly tense. She was worried there wouldn't be enough food to go around, though she could hardly turn people away. I wanted to make myself scarce, but as the bride, that wasn't really an option. What I truly longed for was to be with Dan. We'd be heading back to our mouldy old bedsit after the wedding, but I didn't care. That was ours, our place to begin our new life together. Dad was outside decorating the car for the big day, carefully tying on the bows and ribbons. The car was brand new, and while I can't remember the make, it looked the part. I think he was originally meant to pick up Dan, but with Dan's parents stepping in last minute, Dad had lost that particular role. Decorating the car was his way of still being involved, still contributing. I went out to find him and saw him standing there, fussing over the final touches. He looked up and asked, "What do you think?" I ran over, hugged him, and thanked him for everything, for his support, for helping to organise it all, and especially for paying. He hugged me back and held me a little tighter, mindful of the baby.

Before I knew it, it was time to go. I got into the car with Dad; Pat, my brother-in-law, was driving us. As we pulled away, Dad leaned over, kissed me gently, took my hand, and said, "Are you ready?" I nodded, holding back tears. I didn't want to ruin my make-up now. The church wasn't far, just two miles down the road. The journey passed quickly. It wasn't raining, thankfully, but it was a bit blowy and cold. Still, I was relieved we'd be inside for the photos before the weather had a chance to turn. As we approached, I heard the church bells ringing, and a wave of emotion washed over me. This was it; it was really happening. I felt amazing. I couldn't wait to see Dan.

And there he was. Outside the church.

Dad frowned. "He should be inside; you're not supposed to see each other before the ceremony."

But Dan wasn't following tradition. He wasn't taking no for an answer. In his hand was a single rose and a small box of chocolates.

"Mandy," he said, stepping forward, "I need to speak to you quickly. I'm sorry, but I have to do this."

I was taken aback, unsure of what he was about to say. But the rose reassured me. He hadn't changed his mind.

"You look amazing," he said softly. "Beautiful. I just wanted to give you this gift and let you know you've made me the happiest man alive today. Thank you, Mandy. I must go now, but I can't wait to put that ring on your finger." He winked and turned away. His brother-in-law would be giving him away.

I swallowed hard, willing myself not to cry. I looked up at Dad, who could see the emotion written across my face. He smiled gently. "Are you ready?" he asked again. Just then, the vicar stepped out of the church.

"I have to ask," he said. "Are you sure you want to do this today? It's not too late to change your mind."

Because of my age, the church had only granted permission for the wedding once my parents had signed written consent. I looked him in the eye.

"Yes," I said firmly. "I'm happy. I'd like to continue."

At that moment, the bells rang out again, this time playing the traditional wedding music. I felt like a million dollars. Dad opened the church door, and there was Dan, waiting for me. He smiled, and with every step I took, his grin grew wider. He was tall, stooping slightly, and I found the gesture endearing. He looked incredible, like the man of my dreams. My Dan. My hero. We said our vows. We kissed. We signed the register, and then came the flash of cameras from every direction. We were led outside the church, then across the road for more photographs. To be honest, I wasn't enjoying that part. The cold was getting to me, and it all felt more hectic than I'd imagined.

They were trying to get a photo with the church as a beautiful backdrop, but the veil kept catching on a nearby bush. I, for one, had had enough. I didn't care about the flipping photo; I just wanted to be at the reception, celebrating with my new husband and all our guests. At last, the photo shoot ended, and we made our way to the car together. The venue was only about half a mile away, so before we knew it, we were surrounded by people once more. Dan and I exchanged a knowing glance; we both longed for a moment alone, just the two of us, for what felt like the first time in forever. I suddenly whispered, "How was your dad?" Dan took my hand and said, "He is okay. He really has not said anything now; he knows my wishes; he is happy for us both. Also, he has talked about getting me an interview in the print trade which will set us up for life. Where I can truly look after you, the way you deserve."

"Honestly, it will all be good, I promise. It is getting good isn't it, Dan?" I whispered to him. He replied, "It will get better than this for sure, I promise you everything life has and more." Just as he finished speaking, the car came to a stop. A crowd was already gathered outside, waiting for us. They weren't allowed inside until we had arrived, and as I stepped out, I spotted the photographer again. Oh no, not more photos, I thought. He wanted one of us arriving with our friends to greet everyone. I had invited a small group of close school friends for the day. They were only sixteen, so I imagine it must have felt quite surreal attending a friend's wedding. After the photo, we went inside, where glasses were being prepared for the toast. My dad was due to speak, as was Dan's best man. Dan's father hadn't offered to say anything, although he looked quite comfortable among the guests.

When my dad stood up to speak, he smiled and said, "I have a surprise for Dan and Mandy. They don't know about this part." Dan and I exchanged puzzled glances, shaking our heads, neither of us had a clue what was coming.

Dad continued, "They think they're going back to their flat tonight, but they're not. They're going to Dibden Manor for the night!"

A wave of excitement filled the room, followed by applause. "Wait a minute," he said, raising a hand. "It doesn't stop there." The room fell quiet again. "Tomorrow, they're being taken to the airport and flown to Menorca, Spain, for a week, with spending money. A proper wedding night, and then a real honeymoon."

We were stunned, completely overwhelmed. We hadn't expected anything like this, and we felt utterly overjoyed. A holiday! Dad had even arranged Dan's annual leave without him knowing. It truly felt like our lives were taking their first real step towards lasting happiness.

That wedding night felt a little strange. Even though we had lived together, this felt different, more formal, more meaningful. I wasn't quite sure how to act. Being the young couple we were, we ended up sitting on the bed watching Cagney & Lacey, munching on the snacks Mum had packed for us. At one point, I went to use the bathroom and accidentally burnt my bottom on the towel rail, it was far too hot! It left a nasty red mark, but I honestly didn't care. I was too happy. I'd never stayed in such a posh hotel before. When packing for the night, I had thrown all my things into a Co-op bag, and Mum had scoffed at me. "You can't take that," she'd said, replacing it with a proper holdall that did look far more suitable. Dan and I soon realised we hadn't packed for the holiday, but of course, my parents had already thought of that. We weren't flying out until the day after next, they'd left us a day in between to relax, collect our things, and spend one quiet night at home together. They wanted us to choose our own clothes, knowing how particular I could be.

Chapter 18: It Is How You

Finish

By this point, I had stopped working. My employer had asked me to climb a ladder, something I flatly refused to do while pregnant. When I told Dan, he insisted I give up the job altogether. He didn't think it was fair to put me or the baby at risk. He believed we'd manage without my income, and he was right. It hardly made a difference, as housing benefit covered the rest. Of course, we never intended to rely on benefits long term. Dan was getting into the print trade, and we were determined to support ourselves. We saw the help as a stepping stone, exactly what it was meant to be. My parents had done the same when they started out, and now they were doing very well for themselves. To me, it seemed a perfectly normal way to begin: start where you must, and build towards your own home and future.

As we travelled to our apartment by coach, the sun was shining brilliantly in the sky. The atmosphere was lively; people were chatting excitedly, commenting that it was the best weather they'd had in weeks. The heat was intense, but thankfully the coach was air-conditioned; otherwise, I would have been far too hot. We passed several homes with missing windows and unfinished roofs. The coach driver explained that once a house was fully completed, the owners were required to start paying taxes. It struck us as odd that people would choose to live in incomplete homes, but it seemed to be a common practice; many of the houses we passed appeared unfinished.

As we neared the coast, the scenery grew even more beautiful. The water looked incredibly inviting. Still, I hadn't brought any swimwear; being pregnant, I didn't feel comfortable showing off my newly changing body. I had never felt particularly confident in my figure even before, and now I simply didn't care much about it, though I still didn't want it on display. What mattered most to me was that Dan loved me, and that was more than enough.

The coach finally reached our destination. It was more built-up than I'd expected but still really lovely, with the sun still bright in the sky. We were both quite tired, so we agreed to explore the town the following day. For now, we just wanted to settle into our room and unpack. We enjoyed simply being together. Later, we went downstairs, grabbed some hot dogs, and played a few games of pool. There were other people our age staying at the hotel, and Dan began chatting to them while they played. I left him to enjoy himself and wandered off for a bit of a look around. As I walked away, I suddenly realised I hadn't put on any deodorant; I felt sweaty and self-conscious. I rushed back to the room for a quick shower to freshen up. But as I turned a corner, my foot slipped. I felt myself falling, my leg twisted awkwardly, my knees hit the ground, and then my stomach slammed into the floor. For a moment, I couldn't breathe. I lay there, stunned, unsure if I should move. A wave of panic washed over me. Was the baby okay? I'd landed hard. All I wanted in that moment was to be home with my mum and sister. I needed reassurance, someone to tell me everything would be alright. I was halfway through my pregnancy now. Was she safe? Was she hurt?

A thousand thoughts swirled through my mind. But one thing became clear: I needed Dan. I needed him to hold me and tell me it was all going to be okay. I slowly got up, testing my body for any pain. Surprisingly, I felt fine. No aches, no cramps. Still, I forced myself to walk slowly, replaying the moment in my mind and scolding myself for rushing. Why had I been in such a hurry? It felt foolish now. Back in the room, I showered, put on some deodorant, and got dressed. My stomach still felt normal, no pain, no tension. But she hadn't moved. That worried me more than anything.

When I saw Dan again, he was sitting alone at the bar. I burst into tears the moment I reached him. He pulled me into his arms, asking gently, "What's wrong?" Between sobs, I told him everything. His expression changed at once.

"Has she kicked since you fell?" he asked, and my heart sank as I shook my head.

"I haven't felt her at all."

I could see the concern on his face, though he tried to stay calm. "It'll be okay," he said softly. "I'm sure she's fine."

Still, I knew he was just as worried as I was. The fall had left me shaken. We decided to return to the room and rest before dinner. I ended up falling asleep, not surprising, since pregnancy made me so tired all the time. I hadn't actually been sick since the wedding, which felt like a relief, even though I still had waves of nausea now and then. When I woke up, I felt a sudden rush of joy, she was moving! She gave a series of strong kicks, as if to reassure me she was alright. I smiled and reached for Dan's hand, placing it on my belly in the hope that he would feel her too.

He gasped. "I felt her! I felt her!"

He repeated it with such excitement and awe. It was the first time he had ever felt her kick. Up until then, her movements hadn't been strong enough to be noticeable from the outside. After the fall, this moment meant everything. It was as though she was telling us not to worry, to enjoy our holiday, because she was just fine.

The rest of the honeymoon was mostly rainy, right up until the final day, which greeted us with bright sunshine, just like the day we had arrived. Despite the weather, I had a lovely time with Dan. We cherished spending every moment together. Still, a part of us was ready to return home and begin our new life as a married couple. Once we were back, Dan spoke with his dad, who had helped arrange a job interview for him. Everything seemed to be falling into place, and we were both genuinely excited about the future. It really felt as though life was starting to work out in our favour. At home, we quickly settled back in and got everything organised. Dan went for the interview in the print trade and, not long after, we received brilliant news: he had secured an apprenticeship. Not only that, but they were offering him double his current pay during training.

Once qualified, his salary would be significantly higher. My dad even commented that it was more than they earned at Esso, which was considered a very good wage. Financially, things were beginning to look very promising. With those figures, my dad was confident we'd be able to buy a house in just two years. That kind of future felt within reach now. Dan handed in his notice and accepted the new job. It was a major step forward, and it made us even more excited about the arrival of our baby. Yes, we would still need to rent for another year or so, but after that, we could afford our own place. Even a small flat would be enough, it would be ours, and that meant a lot. It would also mean no more sharing, which was a definite improvement.

Our landlord had mentioned that once the baby arrived, he would move us into another flat where children were allowed, as they weren't permitted in the one we were currently in. The new flat was closer to my parents, and I felt the area was much nicer; it wasn't on a council estate, which gave me peace of mind. It all felt like it was finally coming together, and I was genuinely happy. For the first time in a long while, I could see light at the end of what had been a very dark tunnel. I was married, happily so, and we were steadily building our life together, working hard towards our goals and doing our best to give our baby the best possible start in life. I already knew how deeply I would love and care for her. I could feel the love growing stronger with each passing day. She became my priority in every decision Dan and I made. We were going to be alright. Time flew by as we busied ourselves preparing for her arrival. We didn't actually know for certain if we were having a girl, but

I had a strong feeling; I felt like I already knew her. It was as if she were in there, waiting for me just as much as I was waiting for her. Time seemed to fly by, and before long, the sickness returned, not as badly as before, but it made its presence known. I was only being sick once a day now, and sometimes I managed to avoid it altogether. I was nearly due, and my stomach was enormous. Dan was working long hours while still training, though he had booked two weeks off for when the baby arrived. He had started driving again, and we had bought a car, not a new one, but a reliable vehicle. He felt proud being able to drive me to the antenatal classes. It was getting so close now that some people had already disappeared from the sessions, their babies having arrived before the course had ended.

We were learning breathing techniques, which I knew I'd need. My sister had talked me into giving birth at Hythe, a small cottage hospital and I had agreed and signed up. What Suzanne failed to mention, however, was the crucial detail that Hythe didn't offer pain relief. Oh my word. "Too late," Suzanne said. "You have signed up now, but you will be fine with gas and air."

I wasn't entirely sure about it, but I thought it would at least be convenient for Dan, especially since we were still living in Hythe at the time. So I let it be and began to prepare myself for gas and air during labour. It was two days before my due date when the pain in my back began. It was more than a dull ache; it was constant and getting worse. I wanted to see the doctor just to get checked out, but I had an antenatal appointment booked for the following day. Dan convinced me to wait until then. That night, I barely got any sleep. The pain in my back became seriously intense.

Strangely, I didn't feel anything in my stomach, just a deep, persistent ache in my lower back. It was so bad that even moving around had become a struggle. Thankfully, the sickness I'd experienced earlier in the pregnancy had subsided a couple of weeks prior. The next morning, I waited for Mum and Suzanne to pick me up, and I asked them to take me to the local hospital instead; I didn't feel I could wait for the antenatal appointment any longer. When we arrived, we sat in the waiting area, and my sister remarked that it would probably be a long wait. "It won't come anytime soon," she said. I quickly responded, "Well, I've been in pain all night!"

To our surprise, the midwife called me through quite quickly. After checking me over, she explained that I had started labour; I was one centimetre dilated. However, she said it was still early days and that it would be quite some time yet. She advised me to go home and rest until my contractions were coming every five minutes. I tried to explain that the pain I was feeling wasn't in regular waves; it was just a constant ache in my back, which made it hard to know when a contraction was starting or ending. She reassured me that this could happen and encouraged me to try and stay calm. Suzanne then suggested I go back to her house, and she would run me a bath. I liked the sound of that, especially since I hadn't had a proper bath in a while due to only renting a place. I leapt at the offer, hoping it might help ease the pain in my back.

When we arrived at her house, Suzanne went upstairs to run the bath and then called me up. She said she'd make me a cup of tea and bring some biscuits too. I agreed, feeling a little spoilt and very grateful. She left me alone to get into the bath, and as I was pulling my pants down, I suddenly noticed a blob of bloody jelly running down my leg. Panic hit me instantly. I was frightened and immediately thought something might be wrong with the baby.

I shouted for Suzanne, urging her to come up straight away and look at it. She called back, "It'll be a show, don't worry, it's just the plug coming out, getting ready for the baby to come."

But I wasn't convinced. I needed her to see it for herself and tell me that it was definitely nothing to worry about. I kept calling her, needing the reassurance only she could give in that moment. Eventually, she came upstairs to calm me down. When she saw it, she said, "Yes, it is only your plug. It just means the labour is going the right way and the baby is on the way!"

My baby is on the way. I thought I felt like all my dreams all my wishes had come true in that moment. I was the luckiest girl alive!

I look forward to you joining me for the birth of the second book! I hope you are looking forward to it, as much as I am looking forward to you joining me in the experience. Until then, I leave you with the labour of my love!

Printed in Dunstable, United Kingdom